Imposter Syndrome Decoded

The Complete Guide to Silencing Your Inner Critic, Mastering Your Mindset, and Embracing Your Authentic Self

© Copyright 2024 - All rights reserved.

The content contained within this book may not be reproduced, duplicated or transmitted without direct written permission from the author or the publisher.

Under no circumstances will any blame or legal responsibility be held against the publisher, or author, for any damages, reparation, or monetary loss due to the information contained within this book, either directly or indirectly.

Legal Notice:

This book is copyright protected. It is only for personal use. You cannot amend, distribute, sell, use, quote or paraphrase any part, or the content within this book, without the consent of the author or publisher.

Disclaimer Notice:

Please note the information contained within this document is for educational and entertainment purposes only. All effort has been executed to present accurate, up to date, reliable, complete information. No warranties of any kind are declared or implied. Readers acknowledge that the author is not engaged in the rendering of legal, financial, medical or professional advice. The content within this book has been derived from various sources. Please consult a licensed professional before attempting any techniques outlined in this book.

By reading this document, the reader agrees that under no circumstances is the author responsible for any losses, direct or indirect, that are incurred as a result of the use of the information contained within this document, including, but not limited to, errors, omissions, or inaccuracies.

Table of Contents

INTRODUCTION 1

CHAPTER 1: THE MASQUERADE OF IMPOSTER SYNDROME: UNVEILING THE HIDDEN SELF 3

UNVEILING IMPOSTER SYNDROME: BEYOND DOUBT AND DECEPTION 4
Recognizing Early Signs and Symptoms 6
CULTURAL AND SOCIETAL INFLUENCES: NAVIGATING THE TERRAIN OF EXPECTATIONS 8
The Self-Worth Connection: Untangling Identity From Achievement 9
Tackling Imposter Syndrome: Our Approach 10
DISTINGUISHING IMPOSTER SYNDROME FROM SELF-DOUBT 11
Self-Doubt vs. Imposter Syndrome 11
The Perfectionism Connection 12
Overcoming Imposter Syndrome Across Life Domains 12
Intersectionality and Imposter Syndrome 13
The Role of Self-Compassion 13
THE IMPACT OF IMPOSTER SYNDROME ON LIFE'S CROSSROADS 14

CHAPTER 2: WHEN DOUBT SHADOWS SUCCESS: THE DEEP IMPACT OF IMPOSTER SYNDROME 17

EXAMINING THE CONSEQUENCES OF IMPOSTER SYNDROME 18
How Doubt Erodes Decision-Making and Confidence 19
NAVIGATING THE IMPACT OF IMPOSTER SYNDROME ON MENTAL AND EMOTIONAL WELL-BEING 20
The Hidden Cost of Constant Doubt 20
A Unified Approach to Mitigating Doubt 22
SELF-SABOTAGING BEHAVIORS IN PROFESSIONAL SETTINGS 23
The Impact of Self-Sabotage on Professional Relationships 23
Power Imbalances and Imposter Behaviors 24
The Role of Mentorship and Sponsorship in Overcoming Doubt ... 25
BUILDING RESILIENCE: OVERCOMING SELF-DOUBT 27
Understanding the Long-Term Impact on Career Trajectories 28
THE PATH FORWARD 30

CHAPTER 3: THE ME I SEE: DISCERNING YOUR INDIVIDUAL IMPOSTER BATTLES 31

SELF-ASSESSMENT AND RECOGNITION 32
- Identifying Patterns 32
- Understanding Triggers 34
- Roots of Insecurities 36
- Life Domain Manifestations 38
- Decision-Making and Goal-Setting 41

DEEPENING UNDERSTANDING AND DEVELOPING RESILIENCE 44
- Understanding Self-Doubt and Self-Esteem 45
- The Evolving Nature of Doubts 45
- Embracing Vulnerability 46

EMPOWERMENT THROUGH SHARED EXPERIENCES AND CULTURAL INSIGHT 47

CHAPTER 4: BEHIND THE CURTAIN: DECODING SOCIETAL BLUEPRINTS 49

EXPLORING SOCIETAL NORMS AND EXPECTATIONS 50
- Cultural Contributions to Feelings of Inadequacy 50

INFLUENCE OF GENDER STEREOTYPES 52
- The Pervasive Impact of Gender Stereotypes 52

CHALLENGING SOCIETAL EXPECTATIONS 55
- Redefining Norms 55

BUILDING RESILIENCE AGAINST EXTERNAL PRESSURES 58
- Cultivating Resilience Through Artistic Expression 58

EMPOWERMENT AND COMMUNITY SUPPORT 59
- Creating Transformative Environments 60
- Addressing Mental Health Within Societal Frameworks 60
- Inspiration From the Frontlines of Change 61

CULTIVATING A CULTURE OF EMPOWERMENT 61

CHAPTER 5: BREAKING BARRIERS: DISMANTLING SELF-IMPOSED LIMITATIONS 63

TECHNIQUES TO IDENTIFY AND CHALLENGE NEGATIVE SELF-TALK 64
- Cognitive Restructuring Exercises 64
- Affirmations and Mindset Shifts 64
- Recognizing and Reframing Self-Limiting Beliefs 65

STRATEGIES FOR OVERCOMING PERFECTIONISTIC TENDENCIES 66
- Recognizing and Reducing Perfectionism 66

THE ROLE OF FEAR AND PAST EXPERIENCES 68
- Understanding the Impact of Fear 68

The Influence of Childhood Experiences 69
THE POWER OF POSITIVE AFFIRMATIONS AND SELF-COMPASSION 71
Cultivating a Positive Self-Image With Affirmations 71
Developing Personalized Plans to Overcome Limiting Beliefs 72
FOSTERING LIFELONG GROWTH AND COMMUNITY SUPPORT 73

CHAPTER 6: CELEBRATING YOU: ILLUMINATING YOUR ACHIEVEMENTS 75

BUILDING A PORTFOLIO OF ACHIEVEMENTS 76
Documenting Your Successes Strategically 76
Valuing Your Skills and Contributions 76
TOOLS FOR REFRAMING ACCOMPLISHMENTS 78
Positive Reframing Techniques 78
NAVIGATING SELF-DOUBT IN CAREER ACHIEVEMENTS 79
The Role of Acknowledgment and Validation 80
Setting Realistic Expectations 81
NAVIGATING DOUBTS IN PERSONAL RELATIONSHIPS 82
Building a Supportive Community 82

CHAPTER 7: CULTIVATING SELF-COMPASSION 85

CORE COMPONENTS OF SELF-COMPASSION 86
PRACTICAL EXERCISES FOR CULTIVATING SELF-COMPASSION 87
Mindfulness Techniques 87
Guided Meditations 88
ADDRESSING EMOTIONAL BARRIERS: GUILT, SHAME, AND SELF-DOUBT 89
Understanding Guilt and Shame 89
CULTIVATING A MINDSET OF KINDNESS AND UNDERSTANDING TOWARD ONESELF 91
Cultivating Resilience Through Self-Compassion 91
TOOLS FOR INTEGRATING SELF-COMPASSION INTO DAILY ROUTINES AND HABITS 93
ADDRESSING SELF-CARE IMBALANCES WITH SELF-COMPASSION 94
THE ROLE OF SELF-COMPASSION IN FOSTERING RESILIENCE AND EMOTIONAL STRENGTH 96

CHAPTER 8: CRAFTING YOUR CIRCLE: KNITTING TOGETHER A NETWORK OF AUTHENTIC ALLIES 99

CULTIVATING CONNECTIONS: OVERCOMING DOUBTS TOGETHER 100
Empowering Networks: The Power of Diverse and Inclusive Support 101
FOSTERING TEAM RESILIENCE AND CONNECTION: A COMPREHENSIVE APPROACH 103
Creating a Supportive Professional Environment 104

    Strategies for Effective Mentor-Mentee Relationships *105*
    Navigating Team Dynamics and Power Imbalances *106*
  CULTIVATING COMMUNITY AND FOSTERING BELONGING IN THE WORKPLACE ... 107
    Strategic Implementation of Inclusive Practices *107*
    Structured Mentorship Programs *107*
    Team-Building for Stronger Connections *108*
    Encouraging Collaborative Work Environments *108*
    Understanding and Addressing the Impacts of Impostor Syndrome
    .... *108*
    Integration Through Educational Workshops *109*

CHAPTER 9: BLUEPRINTING SUCCESS: NAVIGATING THE PATH TO YOUR AMBITIONS **111**

  ESTABLISHING A FOUNDATION FOR SUCCESS 112
    Defining Success: A Personalized Approach *112*
  NAVIGATING THE PATH TO YOUR AMBITIONS: OVERCOMING PROCRASTINATION
  AND SELF-DOUBT 115
    Visualization: A Tool for Clarity and Manifestation *116*
  TACKLING IMPOSTER SYNDROME AND THE FEAR OF FAILURE 117
    Creating a Roadmap: Guiding Your Journey *117*
    Fostering Resilience and Determination *118*
    Embracing Adaptability in Goal Pursuit *119*

CHAPTER 10: REFRAMING FAILURE: A JOURNEY THROUGH RESILIENCE AND REINVENTION **121**

  REFRAMING FAILURE AS A STEPPING STONE TO SUCCESS 122
    Learning from Setbacks: A Tactical Approach *122*
  RISK-TAKING AMIDST IMPOSTER SYNDROME 124
    Understanding the Connection Between Imposter Syndrome and
    Risk-Taking *125*
  EMBRACING FAILURE: A CATALYST FOR GROWTH AND INNOVATION 126
    Fostering Self-Compassion in Professional Contexts *127*
    A Pathway to Empowered Resilience *129*

CHAPTER 11: FOSTERING HARMONY BETWEEN AMBITION AND WELL-BEING **131**

  THE DELICATE BALANCE: AMBITION AND IMPOSTER SYNDROME 132
    Navigating Imposter Syndrome in Pursuit of Work-Life Balance. *132*
  IMPOSTER SYNDROME IN CAREER ASPIRATIONS: BRIDGING SELF-DOUBT WITH
  SUCCESS 135
    Strategic Self-Acknowledgment and Visualization *136*

 Cultivating an Achievement-Oriented Mindset 136
 Expanding Professional Development 136
 Adaptive Resilience Practices 137
 Networking and Collaborative Achievements 137
 Rising Above 138

CHAPTER 12: CULTIVATING LASTING CONFIDENCE AND DYNAMIC GROWTH 139

 Creating a Long-Term Plan for Self-Confidence 140
  Dynamic Goal Setting 140
  Cultivating Effective Feedback Loops 141
  Integrating Self-Reflection and Adaptation 141
 Ongoing Practices for Maintaining a Positive Self-Image 142
  Integrating Affirmation Routines Into Daily Life 142
 Encouraging Continuous Personal and Professional Development ... 144
  Embracing Lifelong Learning 144
  Developing Adaptability 145
 Strategies for Sustaining Confidence and Growth Beyond Overcoming Imposter Syndrome 147
  Cultivating Resilience Through Workshops 147
  Enhancing Growth Through Mentorship Roles 148
 Recognizing and Managing the Long-Term Impact of Imposter Syndrome 148
  Strategies for Sustained Growth and Adaptability 149
 Wrapping Up and Looking Ahead 150

CONCLUSION 151

REFERENCES 153

Introduction

The only real mistake is the one from which we learn nothing. –Henry Ford

Imagine standing at a crossroads where each path represents a choice between embracing your true potential and continuing to play a role that no longer resonates with your deeper aspirations. This journey into self-discovery and authentic achievement is not about finding quick fixes but about embarking on a lifelong process of understanding and growth.

The heart of our exploration is the belief that true achievement is not measured by societal benchmarks but by how closely our professional accomplishments and personal development align with our core values. This book is designed to guide you through the process of dismantling the doubts and imposter syndrome that cloud your achievements and obscure your true capabilities.

In *Imposter Syndrome Decoded*, we delve into strategies that help transform failures into learning experiences, cultivate resilience, and foster a mindset that views challenges as opportunities for growth. By learning to recognize and embrace your authentic self, you not only enhance your professional effectiveness but also enrich your personal life.

This book will take you through a series of reflections and exercises designed to help you

- understand the root causes and manifestations of imposter syndrome and learn strategies to combat it.

- build resilience by redefining what failure and success mean to you personally.

- develop practical skills for aligning your daily actions with your long-term goals.

- create an environment that nurtures continuous growth and encourages you to thrive amidst adversity.

As you engage with these pages, you are invited to reflect on your own experiences, challenge your preconceptions, and apply the insights in ways that are most meaningful to your personal and professional journey. Each chapter builds on the previous one, creating a comprehensive path that leads from self-doubt to self-assurance, from external validation to internal fulfillment.

This is not just about reading a book; it's about changing how you view success and your role in achieving it. It's about equipping yourself with the knowledge and tools to transform your life's challenges into powerful catalysts for personal and professional growth. So, as we set forth on this journey together, let's embrace the learning process with open minds and the courage to transform our lives profoundly.

Chapter 1:

The Masquerade of Imposter Syndrome: Unveiling the Hidden Self

Picture this: You're in a high-stakes boardroom meeting, the culmination of your latest project's success. Around the table, your colleagues are offering congratulations, with charts and graphs projecting your achievements on the walls. As the praise continues, a nagging question shadows your thoughts: *Do I really deserve to be here?* This scenario captures the essence of imposter syndrome—a relentless mental tug-of-war where you doubt your own accomplishments and feel like a fraud about to be exposed.

Imposter syndrome isn't just occasional self-doubt; it's a persistent shadow over your sense of achievement, making you feel undeserving of your success. It's especially common among women aged 25 to 50, creating an inner conflict between their achievements and their self-perception. Their stories share a theme: a silent struggle against an inner voice that undermines their external accomplishments.

The concept of imposter syndrome was introduced in the late 1970s by psychologists Pauline Rose Clance and Suzanne Imes (Beranek, 2023). They noticed that many high-achieving women couldn't shake off the feeling that they weren't truly competent and had somehow tricked others into thinking they were.

In this chapter, we're going to pull back the curtain on imposter syndrome, examining its layers and how it's become a hidden barrier for many. We'll tackle the myths head-on, revealing that it's more common and impactful than often assumed. Through relatable stories and research, we aim to demystify this syndrome, bringing it into the light.

Our journey will uncover the roots and manifestations of imposter syndrome, connecting personal experiences with broader societal and cultural influences. This exploration is just the starting point, paving the way for understanding how to recognize and address these feelings. We're setting the stage for a deeper dive into strategies that can help turn self-doubt into self-empowerment, guiding you toward a path of recognizing and embracing your true worth.

Unveiling Imposter Syndrome: Beyond Doubt and Deception

Imposter syndrome is a psychological pattern where individuals doubt their accomplishments and fear being exposed as a fraud. Despite evidence of their success, they believe they are not as competent as others perceive them to be. This syndrome is marked by chronic feelings of intellectual fraudulence, fear of failure, and a tendency to attribute success to external factors like luck or timing.

Statistics reveal that imposter syndrome is particularly prevalent among women aged 25-50. Research indicates that up to 70% of people will experience imposter syndrome at some point in their lives, with a significant portion being women in this age group (Beranek, 2023). This data underscores the pervasive nature of the syndrome, cutting across various demographics and professions.

Personal stories from women who have faced imposter syndrome bring depth to these statistics. For example, Sarah, a 35-year-old executive, constantly feels like she doesn't deserve her role, fearing that one day her colleagues will discover she's not as capable as they think. These narratives highlight the internal turmoil faced by individuals despite outward signs of achievement and recognition.

The term "imposter syndrome" was coined by psychologists Pauline Rose Clance and Suzanne Imes in 1978 (Saymeh, 2023). They observed that despite having outstanding academic and professional accomplishments, many women believed they were not bright and had fooled anyone who thought otherwise. This discovery marked a significant milestone in understanding the internal experiences of high achievers who felt like imposters.

Common misconceptions about imposter syndrome include the belief that it is rare, affects only women, or is a sign of modesty. However, it's a widespread issue affecting all genders, and it can lead to significant psychological distress, not merely an expression of humility.

The impact of imposter syndrome on mental health and well-being is profound. Studies show that it can lead to increased stress, anxiety, depression, and burnout. The syndrome often coexists with other mental health issues, creating a vicious cycle of self-doubt and fear of failure. By recognizing and addressing imposter syndrome, individuals can begin to break this cycle, fostering a healthier self-perception and overall well-being.

Recognizing Early Signs and Symptoms

Have you ever felt like you don't quite belong, even when everyone around you thinks you're doing a fantastic job? This feeling often starts subtly—a nagging thought here, a self-doubt there. You might find yourself brushing off compliments, thinking, *If only they knew,* or working tirelessly to cover up what you perceive as your lack of knowledge or skills. These are telltale signs you might be dealing with what's often called feeling like an imposter.

I'll share a personal confession: Writing this book has been a battleground against my own imposter feelings. Questions like, *What makes me think I can do this?* or, *Who's going to listen to me?* frequently haunted my thoughts. What makes me qualified to guide others? These doubts are not just theoretical but are battles I face with every page I write. Let's delve deeper into how this syndrome subtly takes hold and affects various aspects of our lives.

- **Chronic self-doubt:** Imagine a scenario where, despite receiving accolades for your work, a persistent inner voice insists you're not as capable as others think. This thought process is the core of imposter syndrome—a relentless inner critic that undermines your confidence, casting a shadow over every success. No matter the accolades or achievements, they never seem enough to silence the doubt. This ongoing battle can exhaust your mental reserves, leaving you feeling undeserving and fraudulent, trapped in a cycle where success feels like an accident rather than a deserved outcome.

- **Fear of being uncovered:** The dread of being "found out" as a fraud can be all-consuming, casting a long shadow over your daily life. It's like carrying a secret that you fear will be exposed, leading to a loss of respect and recognition from peers and superiors. This fear isn't just about making a mistake; it's about a deep-seated worry that your entire professional and personal identity might be invalidated if people see the "real" you. This constant anxiety can be crippling, affecting decision-making, relationships, and even willingness to take on new challenges or opportunities.

- **Perfectionism:** Perfectionism, often a companion of imposter syndrome, sets an unattainable benchmark for success. It's the belief that there is no room for error and that anything less than perfect is a failure. This mindset can turn every task into a high-stakes operation, where you over-prepare and exert excessive effort, even in areas where you excel. The irony is that the more you strive for perfection, the more elusive it becomes, creating a cycle of frustration and self-reproach.

- **Attributing success to external factors:** When you consistently attribute your achievements to external factors like luck, timing, or assistance from others, you diminish your role in your own successes. This aspect of imposter syndrome convinces you that your accomplishments are not truly yours, that you were simply in the right place at the right time. It's a belief that overlooks the hard work, skills, and dedication you've put into your achievements, leading to a skewed perception of your worth and abilities.

- **Overworking:** In an attempt to counteract perceived inadequacies, overworking emerges as a common response. It's the idea that if you just work harder, put in more hours, and take on more responsibilities, then perhaps you can stave off exposure as an imposter. However, this often leads to burnout, as the goalpost of "enough" keeps moving, and your well-being is sacrificed at the altar to prove your worth.

- **Sabotaging one's success:** Sabotage is a paradoxical element of imposter syndrome, where you might unconsciously undermine your success to avoid the potential of failure or the pressure of high expectations. Procrastination, avoiding challenges, or downplaying your abilities can be manifestations of this self-sabotage. It's a defense mechanism, albeit a counterproductive one, that protects you from the fear of not living up to the imposter image you've internalized.

By understanding these early signs and how they manifest in our lives, we can begin to recognize the patterns and triggers of imposter syndrome. Acknowledging these feelings is the first step toward addressing them and moving toward a healthier self-perception and self-acceptance.

Cultural and Societal Influences:
Navigating the Terrain of Expectations

Our journey through life, shaped by the cultural and societal landscapes we traverse, deeply influences our perceptions of success and failure. In a world where achievements often define personal worth, the pressure to excel becomes a relentless force. This societal push, steeped in the values and norms of our upbringing, crafts a framework within which we measure our own and others' successes.

In professional spheres, particularly those like STEM or leadership roles where competition is fierce and visibility high, the stakes feel even higher. Women in these fields might find themselves under a magnifying glass, their every move scrutinized, driving the need to overachieve just to prove their place. This relentless proving ground can amplify the sense of being an imposter, creating a cycle where the more one achieves, the greater the fear of being unmasked as a fraud.

The Self-Worth Connection: Untangling Identity From Achievement

At the heart of imposter syndrome lies a fragile thread tying self-worth to achievement. This connection, though seemingly logical in a success-oriented society, is fraught with danger. It transforms self-esteem into a fluctuating market, rising and falling with each success and failure.

When self-worth becomes contingent on external achievements, every error or setback takes on monumental proportions, becoming a referendum on one's identity. This precarious linkage sets the stage for a life where one's value feels perpetually in the balance, dependent on the next achievement or the next accolade. It's a life where the authentic self is overshadowed by the trophies of success and where the intrinsic worth of the individual is obscured by the external markers of achievement.

To move beyond the shadows of imposter syndrome, it's essential to redefine the metrics of self-worth and to untangle the deeply knotted ties between our identity and our achievements. Recognizing that our value is not solely predicated on our successes or failures allows us to embrace a more stable and grounded sense of self. In this light, we can see failures as mere events in our journey, not defining markers of our worth, and celebrate successes as milestones, not the sole arbiters of our value.

Tackling Imposter Syndrome: Our Approach

As we venture deeper into this book, we'll embark on a journey to dismantle the façade of imposter syndrome together. Our exploration will be personal and profound, rooted in understanding and actionable strategies. We'll explore how to build the following skills:

- **Acknowledge and name the feelings:** Recognizing and labeling these experiences as imposter syndrome can diminish their power.

- **Shift the mindset:** Transforming the way we think about success, failure, and personal worth is vital. We'll delve into cognitive-behavioral techniques to reframe self-perception.

- **Cultivate self-compassion:** Learning to treat oneself with kindness and understanding, especially in the face of perceived inadequacy, is a powerful antidote to imposter syndrome.

- **Build authentic confidence:** Developing genuine self-confidence based on skills, experiences, and personal values rather than external accolades.

The Role of Storytelling

Stories have the power to connect, heal, and inspire. By sharing personal experiences, we not only validate our feelings but also discover that we are not alone in this struggle. Through storytelling, we can learn from others who have navigated the path of imposter syndrome, gaining insights into how they've overcome these challenges and transformed their self-doubt into self-empowerment.

In essence, this book aims to be a beacon for those navigating the murky waters of imposter syndrome. By integrating personal narratives with evidence-based strategies, we seek to guide you toward a deeper understanding of yourself and how to authentically affirm your capabilities and achievements.

As we journey through this exploration, we'll uncover that imposter syndrome, while challenging, can also be an opportunity for profound personal growth and self-discovery. The aim is not only to dispel the myths and misconceptions surrounding this syndrome but also to empower you to rewrite your narrative into one where you are the deserving protagonists of your success stories.

Distinguishing Imposter Syndrome From Self-Doubt

While self-doubt is a common human experience, imposter syndrome takes this uncertainty to an extreme level, impacting individuals' ability to recognize and accept their accomplishments. Here, we delve into distinguishing between these nuanced feelings, exploring their connection with perfectionism, and proposing strategies for overcoming the deep-seated sense of being an imposter.

Self-Doubt vs. Imposter Syndrome

Self-doubt is a temporary lack of confidence in one's abilities or decisions, often fleeting and situation-specific. It's a feeling that can be easily overcome with evidence of success or through positive reinforcement. Imposter syndrome, however, is more ingrained and persistent. It involves a chronic pattern of doubting one's success and abilities despite external evidence of competence. This syndrome leads individuals to dismiss their achievements as luck, timing, or the result of deceiving others into overestimating their intelligence and abilities.

The Perfectionism Connection

Perfectionism is closely tied to imposter syndrome. Those experiencing imposter syndrome often set exceedingly high standards for themselves—standards that are neither reasonable nor sustainable. When they inevitably fail to meet these standards, it reinforces their feelings of inadequacy and fuels the cycle of self-doubt. This relationship creates a paradox where the strive for perfection becomes both a driver and a consequence of feeling like an imposter, leading to a relentless pursuit of unattainable goals.

Overcoming Imposter Syndrome Across Life Domains

To overcome imposter syndrome, it's essential to apply strategies across various life domains:

1. **Professional:** Recognize and document achievements, seek feedback, and set realistic goals. Engaging in mentorship can provide perspective and validation of one's skills and contributions.

2. **Personal:** Foster self-awareness to identify imposter thoughts and counter them with rational, positive affirmations. Developing hobbies or interests outside of work can also bolster self-esteem.

3. **Social:** Building supportive relationships where open discussions about feelings of inadequacy are encouraged can diminish the syndrome's impact.

Intersectionality and Imposter Syndrome

Imposter syndrome does not exist in a vacuum; it intersects with various aspects of identity, such as race, gender, sexuality, and socioeconomic status. For example, individuals from underrepresented or marginalized groups might experience these feelings more intensely due to external biases and stereotypes. Recognizing the multifaceted nature of imposter syndrome is crucial in addressing it effectively, as solutions must be tailored to unique experiences and backgrounds.

The Role of Self-Compassion

Self-compassion is a critical tool in combating imposter syndrome. By treating oneself with kindness, understanding, and forgiveness, individuals can alleviate the harsh self-judgment that fuels their imposter feelings. Practicing self-compassion involves recognizing that perfection is unattainable and that mistakes and setbacks are part of the human experience. This mindset shift can help accept the imperfections and value their progress and efforts, regardless of the outcome.

In summary, distinguishing imposter syndrome from self-doubt, understanding its relationship with perfectionism, and applying targeted strategies can significantly alleviate its impact. Recognizing the intersectional nature of these feelings and fostering self-compassion are vital steps in the journey toward overcoming the pervasive sense of being an imposter.

The Impact of Imposter Syndrome on Life's Crossroads

As we journey through the corridors of our professional lives, it's not uncommon to find ourselves at a crossroads where the path ahead seems shrouded in doubt. These moments of hesitation, often brushed aside as mere nervousness, might actually stem from a deeper, more persistent voice that questions our worth and capabilities. It's like walking through a familiar landscape yet feeling inexplicably out of place, as if, at any moment, someone might point out that you don't belong.

Think about the times you've hesitated before stepping into a new role or shied away from opportunities that seemed just within reach. Was it merely a lack of confidence, or was there a lurking fear that success would only amplify your perceived inadequacies? This internal conflict can turn even the most straightforward decisions into a battlefield of self-doubt.

In the sphere of leadership, doubts can cloud judgment and dim the guiding light we're meant to be for others. True leadership isn't about never faltering but about navigating these challenges with courage, authenticity, and transparency. Openly communicating your struggles can foster trust and encourage a culture of openness and collaboration. This transparency in leadership helps demystify decision-making and shows that challenges are opportunities for growth, not just obstacles.

The workplace, especially one riddled with power imbalances, can often feel like a stage where we're constantly performing, trying to prove our worth. But imagine transforming these environments into spaces where everyone's contributions are acknowledged, where success isn't a competition but a shared journey. It's about dismantling the structures that feed our self-doubt and creating a culture of equity and respect.

At the heart of this is our self-esteem, intricately woven into our professional identity. Every decision, achievement, or failure feels like a reflection of our self-worth. Yet, by redefining how we view these experiences—not as judgments but as opportunities for growth—we can begin to forge a professional path that is not only successful but also authentically ours.

And what about the dreams and aspirations we set aside for fear of failing or being exposed? Acknowledging these fears is the first step toward reclaiming the career paths we desire and deserve, paving the way for a life of fulfillment and authenticity.

As we conclude this chapter, we've started to unravel the complex tapestry of doubts that influence our professional decisions and shape our sense of self. But this exploration is far from over. In the next chapter, "When Doubt Shadows Success," we will dive into the profound impact these internal uncertainties have on our lives. We'll see how they can overshadow our achievements and how, by facing these doubts head-on, we can illuminate the path to a future where we confidently own our successes and navigate our world with a renewed sense of purpose and self-assurance.

Chapter 2:

When Doubt Shadows Success: The Deep Impact of Imposter Syndrome

In the first chapter, we unveiled the hidden layers of imposter syndrome, exploring its roots and the silent battle many face in recognizing their own worth. Now, we delve deeper into the profound impacts this syndrome has on those it ensnares. From strained relationships at home to hindered career progression and decision-making paralysis in professional settings, the consequences are far-reaching.

But what makes imposter syndrome particularly insidious is not just the breadth of its impact but its depth. It burrows deep into our mental and emotional well-being, often leading to burnout, diminished self-esteem, and a skewed view of our capabilities and achievements. In this chapter, we explore how these shadows cast by doubt not only obscure our current success but also dim our future aspirations and potential.

Join me as we step out of the shadows and into the light, where success is not just achieved but also believed and embraced. Let's explore how to break free from the chains of doubt and reclaim the confidence and clarity that Imposter Syndrome has long obscured.

Examining the Consequences of Imposter Syndrome

Let's dive into the personal experiences of women who've walked through the shadow of imposter syndrome. Their stories not only shine a light on the struggle but also humanize the profound impacts this syndrome has on both personal and professional realms.

Emily's promotion paralysis captures the essence of imposter syndrome—a fear so intense that it can stop career progress in its tracks. Emily, a high-performing employee at a leading tech firm, found herself paralyzed by doubt when offered a promotion to senior management. Despite years of accolades, she felt unqualified and considered her achievements to be the result of luck rather than skill. This internal conflict led her to initially decline the promotion, showcasing how deeply imposter feelings can affect decision-making.

Sarah's silent struggle reflects another facet of this syndrome. An award-winning architect whose designs have transformed city skylines, Sarah attributes her success to external factors like timing rather than her own talent. Her story highlights how persistent doubts can lead to overworking and burnout, as the fear of being exposed as incompetent drives her to triple-check her work, straining both her health and personal relationships.

Anita's achievement anxiety shows how imposter syndrome can stifle professional growth and self-expression. As a respected university professor frequently invited to speak at international conferences, Anita feels like a fraud. Her fear of public speaking and reluctance to assert her ideas prevent her from seizing opportunities for collaboration and advancement.

These stories are not isolated incidents but common examples of how deeply imposter syndrome can infiltrate the lives of successful women. Each story demonstrates the significant impact of this psychological phenomenon on decision-making and self-confidence.

How Doubt Erodes Decision-Making and Confidence

The reach of imposter syndrome extends deep into the realms of decision-making and self-perception, subtly undermining confidence and altering professional trajectories.

- **Paralysis in decision-making:** For Emily, every decision became a battleground. The fear of being unmasked as a fraud led to hesitation and procrastination. Critical career decisions were deferred or avoided, stunting her professional growth and compounding her feelings of inadequacy.

- **Eroded self-esteem:** Sarah's achievements should have been a source of pride. Instead, her relentless self-doubt turned each accolade into a reminder of her perceived inadequacies. This constant questioning of her worth eroded her self-esteem, making it difficult for her to accept new challenges or seek advancement.

- **Fear-driven performance:** Anita's meticulous preparation for presentations was less about ensuring quality and more about warding off potential criticism. This fear-driven performance restricted her ability to engage freely and creatively in her field, limiting her professional development and personal satisfaction.

- **Stifled professional growth:** The overarching effect of imposter syndrome is a significant dampening of professional potential. It holds individuals back from seizing opportunities, speaking up in key meetings, or pursuing ambitious projects. Instead of a path paved with progressive challenges and growth, it becomes a tightrope walk over a landscape of fears and doubts.

As we dissect these effects, it's clear that overcoming imposter syndrome involves more than just quelling doubts; it requires a foundational change in how we perceive and react to our achievements and failures. By understanding these profound impacts, we can start to develop the tools not just to cope but to thrive.

Navigating the Impact of Imposter Syndrome on Mental and Emotional Well-Being

Imposter syndrome does more than just fill our minds with doubt; it extends its reach into every facet of our lives, affecting our careers, personal relationships, and overall mental health. This relentless pursuit of unrealistic perfection often spirals into burnout, leaving us questioning not only our capabilities but our very worth.

The Hidden Cost of Constant Doubt

Imagine working late into the night, second-guessing every decision you make, or feeling a gnawing anxiety despite receiving praise from your peers and superiors. These scenarios are the reality for many who struggle with this deep-seated doubt. The emotional toll is substantial, leading to burnout—a state of emotional, physical, and mental exhaustion caused by prolonged stress. Burnout goes beyond simple tiredness; it's a comprehensive system shutdown, requiring more than just rest to recover. It calls for a fundamental change in how we perceive and react to our professional roles and personal expectations.

Impacts on Career Progression

For those of us battling these feelings, every professional milestone or opportunity is shadowed by fear—the fear that our achievements are not truly our own but rather the result of luck or external circumstances. This relentless self-doubt can significantly hinder career progression. The pressure to continuously prove ourselves worthy can prevent us from pursuing higher responsibilities or stepping into roles that align with our true potential. Moreover, the fear of exposure as a fraud can make us shy away from opportunities, limiting our professional growth and, ironically, reinforcing the very doubts that hold us back.

Strains on Personal Relationships

The effects of this syndrome extend beyond the confines of our workplaces into our personal lives. The effort to maintain a facade of competence in professional settings can exhaust our emotional reserves, leaving little for personal relationships. This imbalance can strain or sever important personal connections, as we might avoid or pull back from meaningful engagements for fear of being "found out." The emotional toll can manifest in being overly critical or detached, affecting our interactions with family and friends and leading to a cycle of isolation and regret.

Achieving a Balanced Life

Recognizing the need for a balanced approach to work and life is crucial. Setting clear boundaries between professional responsibilities and personal time is a vital step toward sustaining overall well-being. Valuing personal time as much as professional achievements can foster a more fulfilling life where self-worth extends beyond work accomplishments. Moreover, learning to set realistic and achievable goals can help break the cycle of overambition or underachievement fueled by self-doubt. These goals should be challenging yet attainable, providing a sense of accomplishment without the constant pressure of overreaching.

A Unified Approach to Mitigating Doubt

To effectively manage this profound sense of doubt, it's essential to employ a holistic strategy that encompasses both personal well-being and professional fulfillment. Techniques such as mindfulness can stabilize our emotional state, allowing us to approach professional challenges with clarity. Cognitive-behavioral strategies can also be instrumental in transforming negative thought patterns, such as *I must not fail*, into more constructive ones, like *It's okay to make mistakes*.

Creating a supportive work environment is crucial. A workplace culture that encourages open discussions about challenges and vulnerabilities, where successes are celebrated and failures are viewed as growth opportunities, can significantly alleviate the pressures of self-doubt. Such an environment not only assists individuals in managing their feelings of fraudulence but also builds a more empathetic and productive workplace.

This exploration sets the foundation for understanding the broad impacts of deep-seated self-doubt. For a deeper dive into holistic strategies that address both professional and personal aspects, consult the accompanying journal, which features practical tools and detailed discussions designed to help you thrive.

By first comprehending the scope of these issues, we can better appreciate the need for strategies that address both the professional and personal aspects of our lives. As we continue, we will delve deeper into specific techniques and approaches that help manage and overcome these challenges, ensuring that our journey toward success is both achieved and genuinely felt.

Self-Sabotaging Behaviors in Professional Settings

Self-sabotaging behaviors, often stemming from deep-seated self-doubt, can significantly undermine an individual's effectiveness in professional environments. These behaviors not only impact personal career progression but also affect interpersonal relationships and power dynamics within organizations. Understanding these behaviors and their consequences is the first step toward overcoming them and fostering a more supportive and equitable workplace.

The Impact of Self-Sabotage on Professional Relationships

In professional settings, self-doubt often manifests as hesitation to speak up, contribute ideas, or take on leadership roles. This reticence can stem from a fear of being exposed as less competent than others perceive, leading individuals to withdraw and avoid the spotlight. Such behaviors can diminish one's presence and authority, limiting opportunities for career advancement and contributing to a cycle of underachievement and increased self-doubt.

For example, consider a project manager who consistently doubts her decisions and, therefore, hesitates to provide clear direction to her team. This lack of decisiveness can lead to confusion and inefficiency, eroding her team's confidence in her leadership and her own sense of self-efficacy. Over time, this dynamic can strain professional relationships, as colleagues may perceive her as unsure or untrustworthy, further reinforcing her imposter feelings.

Strategies to Enhance Professional Interactions

- **Leadership training:** Engaging in leadership development programs can equip individuals with the tools to assert themselves effectively, make decisive choices, and manage teams with confidence.
- **Regular feedback:** Encouraging a culture of constructive feedback can help individuals understand how their contributions are valued and where they can improve, reinforcing their competence and reducing self-doubt.

Power Imbalances and Imposter Behaviors

The feelings of being an imposter can exacerbate power imbalances within the workplace, especially for those from underrepresented groups who may already face systemic barriers to advancement. When individuals believe they do not deserve their role or accomplishments, they may unconsciously reinforce these imbalances by not pursuing opportunities for growth or leadership.

These power imbalances are particularly detrimental in environments where diversity in leadership is lacking. Individuals who do not see themselves represented in higher echelons may feel their aspirations are unattainable, further discouraging them from stepping into roles that could disrupt these dynamics.

Addressing Power Dynamics

- **Inclusive policies:** Organizations can implement policies that actively promote diversity in hiring and advancement, ensuring that all employees have the opportunity to rise to leadership positions.

- **Empowerment initiatives:** Programs that empower employees to take on challenges and affirm their abilities can help mitigate the effects of self-doubt and promote a more balanced representation in power structures.

The Role of Mentorship and Sponsorship in Overcoming Doubt

Mentorship and sponsorship are invaluable in helping individuals recognize and combat imposter feelings. A mentor serves as a guide and confidant, offering advice and support based on their own experiences, which can demystify the path to success and alleviate feelings of isolation (*How Can External Support and Mentorship Help You*, 2019). Sponsors can play an even more active role by advocating for an individual's promotion and inclusion in high-value projects, which directly counteracts the imposter narrative by validating the individual's worth and capabilities in visible and impactful ways.

For instance, a young engineer might feel overwhelmed and underqualified in her new role at a large tech company. A mentor could help her navigate these feelings by sharing their own experiences of overcoming similar challenges, while a sponsor might ensure she is included in key meetings and projects, boosting her visibility and confidence.

Enhancing Mentorship and Sponsorship

- **Structured mentorship programs:** Organizations should consider establishing formal mentorship programs that match less experienced employees with seasoned professionals.

- **Active sponsorship:** Leaders can be encouraged to not just mentor but actively sponsor promising employees, advocating for their advancement and exposure within the company.

By weaving together these strategies, organizations and individuals can address the pervasive issue of self-sabotage in professional settings. The goal is to create environments where self-doubt is met with support, not stigma, where achievements are recognized as the result of ability and effort, and where every employee is empowered to pursue their fullest potential without the shadow of imposter syndrome.

This comprehensive approach not only helps individuals overcome personal barriers but also contributes to a more dynamic, inclusive, and effective organizational culture. It's about transforming not just individual trajectories but reshaping the very dynamics that define professional success and fulfillment.

Building Resilience: Overcoming Self-Doubt

Building resilience against the persistent whispers of self-doubt that characterize imposter syndrome is not just about personal triumph; it's about creating environments and cultures that support every professional's potential, regardless of their field. By examining real-life success stories, understanding the long-term impact of imposter feelings on career trajectories, and implementing field-specific strategies, individuals can find the confidence to embrace their achievements and aspire to higher goals.

Dr. Lena's journey is particularly inspiring. A biomedical researcher, she navigated a field where she felt overshadowed by her male counterparts. Despite her early successes, lingering doubts about her belonging and worth persisted. Through engaging with a mentor and participating in leadership development, Lena began to truly own her accomplishments. Now, she not only leads her own research team but also mentors young women entering the field, creating a supportive space for them to grow without the burden of self-doubt.

Similarly, Rachel, a software engineer, transformed her struggle with imposter feelings into an opportunity for organizational change. After recognizing that many of her colleagues shared her insecurities, she initiated workshops on confidence building and effective communication. These sessions have helped many to overcome their doubts and have fostered a culture of openness and support within her tech company.

Understanding the Long-Term Impact on Career Trajectories

Imposter syndrome can significantly alter the course of one's professional journey. Without intervention, the constant self-doubt and fear of exposure can prevent even the most talented individuals from pursuing higher roles or seizing opportunities that match their abilities (Ramaswamy, 2023). It's crucial for professionals to recognize the signs early and seek appropriate support. Being open about their feelings, actively seeking feedback, and engaging in continuous professional development are critical steps in mitigating the effects of imposter syndrome.

For example, career progression often hinges not just on one's current performance but also on one's vision for their future. Individuals bogged down by imposter feelings may set their career aspirations too low, unwittingly stifling their growth. Conversely, by addressing these feelings, professionals can set more ambitious goals and pursue them with conviction, leading to a more fulfilling and successful career.

Tailoring Strategies to Combat Imposter Feelings Across Fields

Different professional fields can pose unique challenges that may trigger or exacerbate imposter feelings, necessitating tailored approaches:

- **Academia:** The pressure to publish and secure funding can intensify self-doubt. Academic professionals can benefit from forming support groups that provide a sense of community and collective coping mechanisms. These groups can also serve as a forum for sharing strategies for dealing with the specific pressures of academic work.

- **Corporate sector:** In fast-paced environments such as finance or technology, formal mentorship and sponsorship programs can be particularly effective. These initiatives not only provide support and guidance but also enhance visibility and recognition, crucial elements for overcoming imposter feelings.

- **Creative industries:** In fields where work is subjectively evaluated, such as the arts or advertising, structured feedback sessions can help professionals develop a more objective view of their work. These sessions can foster a better understanding of one's skills and accomplishments, countering the subjective criticisms that fuel imposter syndrome.

Implementing these strategies requires commitment from both individuals and organizations. Workshops that focus on skill development—such as public speaking, leadership, and stress management—can be integrated into professional development programs. Moreover, promoting a culture that values open dialogue about imposter feelings can demystify these experiences and reduce their stigmatization.

By weaving together these narratives and strategies, the goal is to empower professionals to navigate their careers without being hindered by unfounded doubts. Each success story, strategy, and supportive measure builds on the last, creating a comprehensive approach to fostering resilience. This not only helps individuals overcome personal barriers but also contributes to a more dynamic, inclusive, and effective professional environment. Ultimately, overcoming imposter syndrome is about moving beyond individual successes to foster a culture where all can thrive, confident in their skills and right to belong.

The Path Forward

In this chapter, we've journeyed through the often challenging landscape of imposter syndrome, understanding its deep impact on our professional lives and personal well-being. We've seen how pervasive self-doubt can stifle our potential and learned through inspiring success stories that these feelings can indeed be overcome with the right support and strategies.

By engaging with mentorship, embracing supportive environments, and adopting tailored strategies, we can begin to dismantle the barriers erected by our own doubts. This path isn't just about professional development—it's about personal liberation from the fears that hold us back from embracing our full capabilities.

As we turn the page to the next chapter, we'll dive into a more introspective exploration. This next chapter promises a candid look into recognizing and understanding the unique contours of our own imposter syndrome. It's about shifting our perspective inward to better understand how these feelings of fraudulence are personally crafted and how they affect our daily lives.

Join me as we continue to peel back the layers of doubt and self-deception, moving toward a more authentic and empowered self-understanding. Let's explore the personal battles with imposter syndrome, not just to fight them but to truly see ourselves beyond the shadows of doubt.

Chapter 3:

The Me I See: Discerning Your Individual Imposter Battles

In the labyrinth of our professional lives, a subtle yet pervasive voice often whispers doubts into our ears, casting shadows over our achievements and amplifying our insecurities. This voice, rooted deeply in what many call imposter syndrome, challenges our sense of belonging and worthiness at every step of our careers. Recognizing and confronting this internal adversary is not just beneficial but essential for personal and professional growth. It begins with a journey of self-assessment and recognition, where we uncover the patterns of doubt that haunt us and learn to appreciate our true capabilities.

To embark on this path, we must first learn to identify the recurring themes in our self-perception. How often have we dismissed our successes as flukes or attributed them to external factors rather than acknowledging our own hard work and talent? Reflecting on these questions helps peel back the layers of doubt and allows us to see a clearer picture of our professional personas. This introspection is crucial—it not only reveals the roots of our insecurities but also sets the stage for transformative growth.

Self-Assessment and Recognition

Many of us carry a whispering voice that undermines our successes and magnifies our fears. This voice feeds on our insecurities, doubts, and the dissonance between our self-perception and the expectations of those around us. To address these challenges, it's crucial to embark on a journey of self-assessment and recognition, where we identify patterns, understand triggers, and confront the roots of our insecurities.

Identifying Patterns

Understanding the nuances of how we perceive ourselves and our accomplishments is a critical step in addressing the underlying self-doubt that can shadow our professional and personal lives. To begin this process, it's essential to recognize the recurring patterns in how we internally process our achievements and the moments when we might undervalue our abilities.

Exploring Self-Perception and Achievement

Reflect on the instances where you've minimized your own successes or credited them to factors outside your control, such as luck or opportune timing. This reflection is not just about acknowledging these moments but understanding their frequency and context. Consider the following questions to guide your introspection:

- **Moments of doubt:** When have I felt least deserving of my accomplishments? Identify specific instances and explore the feelings associated with these moments.

- **Self-minimization:** In what situations have I downplayed my capabilities? Reflect on times when you might have attributed success to external factors or downplayed your role in achieving positive outcomes.

- **External attribution:** How frequently do I credit my successes to external factors rather than my own efforts and decisions? Assess whether there is a pattern in how you perceive your role in your achievements.

By engaging in this reflective exercise, you start to paint a clearer picture of how and when self-doubt creeps into your self-assessment. This awareness is crucial—it forms the bedrock upon which you can build strategies to confront and reshape these perceptions.

Practical Steps for Pattern Recognition

To effectively identify and alter these patterns, consider maintaining a dedicated journal where you can document instances of self-doubt as they occur. This practice can help you build the following skills:

- **Track recurrences:** Keeping a detailed record allows you to see patterns over time, making it easier to identify specific triggers and common themes in your self-doubt.

- **Analyze contexts:** Writing down the circumstances under which you experience these feelings provides insights into the environments or tasks that may exacerbate your doubts.

- **Develop counterstrategies:** Once you recognize the situations and contexts that trigger your self-doubt, you can begin to develop targeted strategies to address them. For instance, if you find that you often feel undeserving during performance evaluations, you might prepare by reviewing your accomplishments in detail before these evaluations, reinforcing your confidence in your contributions.

This methodical approach to identifying and understanding your patterns of self-doubt is not just about improving self-awareness. It's a transformative process that sets the stage for more profound changes in how you view yourself and your achievements, ultimately fostering a healthier, more confident self-perception.

Understanding Triggers

Self-doubt doesn't arise in a vacuum—it's often triggered by specific events or environments. Certain scenarios are particularly potent in igniting self-doubt, typically those involving a significant degree of exposure or pressure. Key situations include these examples:

- **Public accolades:** Recognition, while affirming, can paradoxically invoke fear that one's true capabilities will come under scrutiny and be found wanting.

- **Promotions:** Ascending to a higher role often comes with anxiety about meeting new expectations and proving one's worth in the elevated position.

- **Competitive settings:** Environments that foster direct comparison with peers, such as performance reviews or contests, can heighten feelings of inadequacy and spotlight fears of not measuring up.

These situations can serve as a lens, magnifying every perceived flaw and mistake, thereby intensifying feelings of self-doubt.

Strategies for Managing Triggers

To effectively manage and mitigate these triggers, adopting proactive strategies can provide stability and confidence. Implementing a reflective journal can be particularly beneficial:

1. **Consistent documentation:** Regularly document instances when feelings of doubt arise. Detail the circumstances, your emotional response, and the outcomes of the situation.

2. **Pattern recognition:** Periodically review your journal entries to identify common triggers or recurring themes in your reactions. Recognizing these patterns is crucial for understanding your personal triggers and preparing appropriate responses.

3. **Developing coping strategies:**

    o **Enhanced preparation:** For triggers like public speaking, increase your preparation to boost confidence. Rehearse extensively to feel more in control and reduce anxiety.

    o **Skill building:** Actively seek opportunities to improve skills that relate to your triggers. For example, if leadership responsibilities cause anxiety, pursue leadership training or mentoring.

    o **Seek feedback:** Regularly solicit constructive feedback from trusted colleagues. This feedback can demystify others' perceptions of your work and reduce feelings of being an imposter.

4. **Positive affirmations:** After each instance where you successfully navigate a trigger, record what strategies

helped and how you felt. This positive reinforcement strengthens your self-assurance and gradually shifts your mindset toward confidence.

By recognizing the specific situations that trigger self-doubt and actively applying strategic responses, you empower yourself to navigate these challenges with greater effectiveness. How might your approach to these triggers change if you had a toolkit at your disposal? We delve deeply into detailed strategies and coping mechanisms for managing these triggers in our companion journal. This resource is designed to provide you with additional tools, enhancing your resilience and equipping you to turn these moments of doubt into opportunities for growth.

Roots of Insecurities

Our self-perception and the confidence with which we navigate the world are deeply influenced by the beliefs we've internalized over our lives. The seeds of doubt are frequently sown in early experiences where feedback, whether overtly critical or subtly dismissive, has a profound impact. This might include offhand remarks from a parent praising another child's achievements over yours, a teacher who seemed perpetually unimpressed with your efforts, or a mentor whose expectations seemed impossibly high. These experiences can leave a lasting impression, setting a mental benchmark for comparison and self-evaluation that feels perpetually out of reach.

Reflective Exploration

To begin unraveling these deeply rooted insecurities, engage in a reflective exploration:

- **Early memories:** Recall your earliest experiences where you felt you fell short. What specific instances come to mind? Who was involved, and what was said or implied about your efforts?

- **Influential figures:** Consider the significant people in your early life—parents, teachers, coaches. How did their expectations or criticisms impact your view of your abilities? Reflect on how their attitudes toward success and failure may have influenced your own.

- **Recurring themes:** Identify if there are consistent themes in your insecurities. Do they predominantly relate to certain areas of your life, such as academic achievements, social interactions, or professional milestones? Recognizing these patterns can provide clues to the underlying beliefs that fuel your self-doubt.

Addressing and Reconstructing Beliefs

Understanding the source of your insecurities allows you to begin the process of reconstructing your self-beliefs. This process isn't about erasing past experiences but about reshaping how you interpret them in your current life context. Here are some strategies to consider:

- **Contextual reevaluation:** Place old beliefs in the context of your current achievements and experiences. For instance, a teacher's past criticisms about your work may not hold true against the backdrop of your professional success.

- **Affirmative counterpoints:** For every negative belief, develop a counter-affirmation that highlights your capabilities and successes. If you've believed that you're not a strong public speaker because of early failures, remind yourself of recent times when you effectively communicated your ideas in meetings or presentations.

- **Seek constructive feedback:** Engage with trusted peers or mentors to get a realistic perspective on your skills and achievements. Often, external feedback from colleagues who see your daily contributions can provide a more balanced view than the skewed perceptions rooted in past criticisms.

By methodically examining and addressing the origins of your insecurities, you initiate the process of dismantling outdated beliefs that no longer serve your best interests, paving the way for a more confident and secure self-image. This journey isn't merely about challenging negative thoughts; it's about constructing a foundation of positive self-perception that nurtures your growth and aspirations. What if you could accelerate this transformation? Our companion journal offers a deeper exploration into strategies that reinforce this new foundation, providing step-by-step guidance to foster enduring self-confidence and resilience.

Life Domain Manifestations

Self-doubt does not limit its influence to just one aspect of our lives; rather, it permeates various domains, shaping how we engage with the world around us. From professional environments and academic settings to personal relationships and leisure activities, the impact of self-doubt can be both pervasive and profound. Recognizing how these feelings manifest across different areas of life is crucial for developing targeted strategies to manage them effectively.

Professional Impact

In the workplace, self-doubt often manifests as hesitation or reluctance to pursue advancement opportunities. You might find yourself doubting your qualifications for a promotion or feeling anxious about asserting your ideas in meetings, worried that others might question your competence. This can not only stall your career progression but also limit your contribution to team goals and discussions, affecting both personal growth and the broader organizational success.

Academic Challenges

In academic settings, the pressure to perform and excel can exacerbate feelings of inadequacy. You may question your intellectual abilities, especially when faced with challenging coursework or competitive peers. This can lead to a cycle of stress and underperformance, where the fear of not living up to expectations actually hampers your ability to achieve potential academic success.

Personal Relationships

Self-doubt can also strain personal relationships. The fear that others might see your perceived flaws can prevent you from forming deep and meaningful connections. You might hold back in relationships and be hesitant to fully open up for fear of judgment or rejection. This reluctance to be vulnerable can hinder the development of trust and intimacy, foundational elements of any strong relationship.

Leisure and Social Activities

Even in areas meant for relaxation and enjoyment, such as hobbies or social gatherings, self-doubt can creep in. You might avoid activities where you feel you're not particularly skilled, or you might not participate fully in social events, worried about how others perceive you. This can rob you of the joy and fulfillment that these activities are meant to provide, reinforcing a cycle of withdrawal and missed opportunities for enjoyment and social interaction.

Strategies for Addressing Life Domain Manifestations

Understanding the specific ways in which self-doubt affects different areas of your life is the first step toward mitigating its impact. Here are some strategies to consider:

- **In the workplace:** Actively seek feedback and mentorship to bolster your confidence in your professional capabilities. Engage in skill-building activities that align with your career goals to reduce feelings of inadequacy.

- **In academia:** Set realistic academic goals and celebrate small achievements along the way to build confidence. Engage with supportive peers or study groups that foster a positive learning environment.

- **In personal relationships:** Practice openness and vulnerability in safe, supportive settings to strengthen your relationships. Consider therapy or counseling to explore deeper issues of self-worth and relationship dynamics.

- **In leisure activities:** Choose activities that genuinely interest you, regardless of your skill level, and focus on the enjoyment they bring rather than your performance. Gradually expose yourself to more challenging or public aspects of these hobbies to build confidence in your abilities.

By addressing the manifestations of self-doubt in these varied life domains, you can begin to reclaim your confidence and enjoy a more fulfilling and engaged life. Each step you take to confront and manage these doubts not only improves your current situation but also builds a foundation for future resilience and self-assurance.

Decision-Making and Goal-Setting

Self-doubt can significantly influence how we make decisions and set goals, often leading us down a path of either excessive caution or unrealistic expectations. Understanding this influence is crucial for recalibrating our approaches to decision-making and goal-setting, ensuring they lead to personal and professional growth rather than frustration and stagnation.

The Impact on Decision-Making and Goals

When self-doubt enters the decision-making process, it can cloud our judgment, making it difficult to choose paths that align with our true potential and aspirations. You may find yourself falling into these two patterns:

- **Choosing safer paths:** Opting for goals or decisions that are well within your comfort zone to avoid the risk of failure. While this decision can minimize immediate stress, it may also prevent you from reaching your full potential and experiencing growth.

- **Setting unrealistically high goals:** Conversely, you might set excessively high goals as a way to prove your worth to yourself and others. These goals, often unreachable, can set you up for failure and reinforce feelings of inadequacy.

Strategies for Effective Decision-Making and Goal Setting

To combat the effects of self-doubt on your decision-making and goal-setting, consider implementing the following strategies:

- **Realistic goal setting:**
    - **Assess your abilities:** Start with a realistic assessment of your current skills and resources. This step can help in setting goals that are challenging yet achievable.
    - **Incremental milestones:** Break larger goals into smaller, manageable milestones. Celebrating these smaller successes can build confidence and maintain momentum.
    - **Flexibility:** Allow room for adjustments. Goals should evolve as you gain more insight and experience, not remain static.
- **Developing a robust decision-making framework:**
    - **Seek diverse opinions:** Involve trusted peers or mentors in your decision-making process. They can provide alternative perspectives and valuable insights that might not be evident when self-doubt clouds your judgment.

- **Pros and cons analysis:** For significant decisions, take the time to systematically analyze the benefits and drawbacks. This structured approach can reduce the emotional impact of self-doubt.

- **Reflective practice:** After making a decision, reflect on the process and outcomes. Understanding what worked or didn't work can improve your decision-making skills over time.

- **Regular review and adjustment of goals:**

    - **Periodic reviews:** Set regular intervals to review your goals. This is crucial for ensuring that they still align with your long-term objectives and adjusting them based on new skills, experiences, or changes in circumstances.

    - **Seek feedback:** Regular feedback on your progress can provide objective criteria to measure your success and guide future goal adjustments.

    - **Celebrate achievements:** Recognizing and celebrating achievements can reinforce positive decision-making and goal-setting practices. It helps build a narrative of competence and success, countering the negative self-perceptions that self-doubt can create.

By actively managing how self-doubt influences your decision-making and goal-setting, you can ensure that your choices propel you forward rather than hold you back. Implementing a structured, reflective approach to setting realistic goals and making informed decisions allows you to build confidence and assert control over your professional trajectory and personal growth. This proactive stance empowers you to pursue your aspirations with clarity and confidence, significantly reducing the impact of self-doubt on your path to success.

Tying It All Together

Understanding and overcoming self-doubt requires a holistic approach that considers the varied and interconnected ways in which these feelings manifest. By recognizing the patterns and triggers, addressing the roots of your insecurities, and understanding the influence of societal expectations, you can begin to forge a path toward a more secure and confident self. Here, it's essential to embrace vulnerability, seek understanding, and challenge the internal and external narratives that have held you back. As you work through these strategies, remember that the goal is not to eradicate self-doubt entirely but to manage it effectively, allowing you to move forward with confidence and clarity.

Deepening Understanding and Developing Resilience

Navigating our professional and personal landscapes often involves wrestling with self-doubt and nurturing our self-esteem—two forces that deeply influence our sense of identity and capability. Understanding these dynamics, learning from others' experiences, and embracing our own vulnerabilities are key to building resilience and a more authentic self.

Understanding Self-Doubt and Self-Esteem

Self-doubt and self-esteem are intricately linked, often creating a cyclical relationship that can spiral into persistent feelings of inadequacy. When we constantly question our achievements or feel like we don't truly deserve our successes, our self-esteem takes a hit. This diminished self-esteem feeds back into our self-doubt, perpetuating a cycle that can be difficult to break.

To address this cycle, it's crucial to recognize the triggers and patterns of these thoughts. Do high-stakes situations at work make you feel like you're under a microscope, judged, and possibly exposed? Does receiving praise or promotions trigger a fear that you'll soon be "found out"? Understanding these triggers helps to anticipate and prepare for the emotional responses they provoke.

Breaking the cycle involves challenging our negative thoughts and the assumptions behind them. Techniques like cognitive restructuring, which encourages us to question and reframe our negative beliefs, can be transformative. For example, instead of thinking, *I only got this project because no one else was available*, we might reframe this thought to, *I was chosen for this project because my skills and track record demonstrate I can handle it.*

The Evolving Nature of Doubts

Our self-doubt does not remain static; it evolves as we progress through different stages of our lives and careers. Early in our careers, we might feel unprepared and unskilled. As we gain experience, the nature of our doubts might shift to whether we can continue to adapt and meet new challenges.

Recognizing this dynamic allows us to adapt our coping strategies as our lives change. It's about maintaining a learner's mindset—continuously seeking new knowledge and feedback, which can reinforce our competence and quiet our doubts. This proactive approach keeps our skills sharp and our self-confidence refreshed.

Embracing Vulnerability

One of the most effective ways to combat the paralyzing effects of self-doubt is to embrace vulnerability. Opening up about our insecurities can seem daunting, but it allows us to connect with others on a more authentic level, fostering relationships that support and strengthen us.

Creating environments where vulnerability is seen as a strength rather than a weakness can transform our personal and professional relationships. This might mean initiating conversations about challenges and insecurities at work, or it could involve seeking professional help through therapy or coaching, where vulnerabilities can be explored and understood in a safe space.

By deepening our understanding of how self-doubt interacts with our self-esteem, learning from others, adapting to the changing nature of our challenges, and embracing vulnerability, we build a stronger, more resilient self. These strategies not only help us manage doubts but also enrich our relationships and enhance our overall well-being.

Now, we will expand our focus from internal strategies to external influences. This process will include exploring how societal and cultural factors shape our perceptions and how embracing a shared experience can lead to empowerment and a more profound sense of community. This transition not only broadens our understanding but also connects our personal journeys to larger, communal narratives.

Empowerment Through Shared Experiences and Cultural Insight

In our journey to navigate and transcend the often paralyzing doubts shadowing our achievements, it becomes clear that this isn't just a solitary battle; it's a collective struggle transcending individual experiences. By exploring the shared nature of these challenges and the unique ways they manifest across different cultures, we not only find comfort but also draw powerful strategies for personal empowerment and growth.

Realizing that our personal doubts are part of a universal experience can be profoundly liberating. Whether in high-stakes fields, like technology or academia, or across various stages of our careers, most of us have grappled with feelings of inadequacy at some point. This commonality helps diminish the stigma surrounding these doubts, fostering a supportive atmosphere where discussing these feelings openly is not only possible but encouraged.

The manifestation of these doubts can vary significantly based on cultural backgrounds, gender, profession, and life stage. For example, individuals from underrepresented groups might face an additional layer of challenge, navigating professional fields where few share their background. This can intensify feelings of being an outsider or doubting one's place and contributions.

To illustrate, let's revisit a workshop hosted by Shahroo Izadi, where diverse women shared their struggles with self-doubt. A poignant story emerged from a young professional who described her early career as a mental battleground of unworthiness, overshadowing her achievements. Her relentless quest for external validation was a familiar echo to many at the workshop, highlighting a common pursuit among professionals to silence their internal critics with external approval (*What I'm Struggling With*, 2023).

Emma's journey resonates because it mirrors the transition many seek: moving from external validation to internal affirmation. She started each day by affirming, "I am good at what I do." This simple mantra became a powerful tool in rebuilding her self-esteem and reasserting her professional presence, showcasing the transformative power of embracing and affirming one's worth and capabilities.

Moving Forward: Empowerment and Societal Impact

As we close this chapter, our exploration of shared experiences and cultural insights equips us to face and reshape the narratives that dictate our self-worth. The next chapter will build on this foundation, tackling societal expectations and cultural norms that perpetuate these challenges. By addressing these broader influences, we aim to empower not only ourselves but also advocate for a societal transformation that supports personal and collective growth.

In sum, this chapter doesn't just aim to empower us as individuals; it sets the stage for a broader societal dialogue about how cultural forces shape personal perceptions and professional interactions. By understanding and addressing these dynamics, we prepare ourselves to not only navigate but also transform the societal blueprints that affect us all, paving the way for a future where success is not overshadowed by doubt but illuminated by our true capabilities and achievements.

Chapter 4:

Behind the Curtain: Decoding Societal Blueprints

Imagine navigating a world governed by invisible rules—unseen societal blueprints that outline how you should achieve, act, and feel about your accomplishments and failures. For many women, this isn't a distant concept; it's a daily reality that shapes their experiences in profound and often challenging ways. As we pull back the curtain on these societal forces, we explore how cultural norms and gender stereotypes subtly instill self-doubt and pressure women into conforming to predefined roles.

Why do we adhere to these norms? Often, it's not out of personal agreement but rather a learned response to cultural signals that start influencing us from a young age. These messages about how women should look, behave, and even think permeate from media portrayals, educational materials, and expectations from peers and family. They are not merely external pressures; they internalize as voices, influencing decisions and self-perceptions.

However, by identifying these societal scripts, we gain the power to question and dismantle them. This chapter is not just an exploration—it's a rallying cry to challenge the norms, redefine success on our terms, and empower ourselves and others to move beyond the shadows of doubt to a place of self-assurance and authenticity.

Exploring Societal Norms and Expectations

As we dive deeper into the complexities of societal norms and expectations, it becomes clear that the cultural landscape in which we live plays a pivotal role in shaping our self-view, particularly for women. How might your life change if you could step outside these prescribed roles?

These cultural backgrounds and societal norms, steeped in history and tradition, often carry implicit messages about what is expected of women, both in terms of behavior and achievement. These expectations can significantly contribute to feelings of inadequacy, as they set a bar that many may find unattainable or misaligned with their personal aspirations.

Cultural Contributions to Feelings of Inadequacy

Across different cultures, the role of women has traditionally been framed around certain archetypes, such as the caregiver, homemaker, or supporting figure, rather than the leader or innovator. While these roles are inherently valuable, the issue arises when they are imposed rather than chosen, limiting women's views of what they can aspire to become. This cultural scripting can lead many to feel inadequate when their ambitions or personalities diverge from these traditional roles.

Furthermore, the professional achievements of women are often overshadowed by societal expectations about their personal lives, such as marriage and motherhood. Achievements in the workplace or in public life can be undervalued compared to these traditional milestones, creating a dichotomy between professional success and personal fulfillment. This cultural narrative can diminish the perceived value of professional success, compounding feelings of inadequacy among women who strive for accomplishments outside of these societal norms.

Pressure to Conform

The pressure to conform to these societal standards can be intense and multifaceted. It is not just about achieving a certain status or fulfilling expected roles; it is also about how women should go about these achievements—often with grace, humility, and beauty, regardless of the personal costs. The expectation to seamlessly manage careers, families, and social expectations without faltering sets an almost superhuman standard that can be both exhausting and demoralizing.

In professional settings, this pressure manifests as the need to constantly prove oneself against a backdrop of gender stereotypes that question women's capabilities in leadership roles or in traditionally male-dominated fields. In personal settings, it might appear in the subtle discouragements from pursuing interests or careers deemed "unfitting" for women or in the disproportionate praise received for upholding traditional roles over professional achievements.

The confluence of these pressures creates a pervasive sense of having to live up to an impossible ideal, which is neither fair nor feasible. Breaking free from these molds requires a conscious effort to recognize these pressures, understand their origins, and actively challenge them.

By engaging in discussions about these societal norms and their impact and reflecting on our own experiences and those of others in our community, we can begin to dismantle these outdated structures. This process is not just about rejecting or denouncing cultural norms but about reshaping them to embrace a broader spectrum of aspirations and identities. It's about affirming that women's worth is not tied to how well they fit into precast roles but how authentically they live their truths. Explore our companion journal for a detailed guide on navigating and reshaping these societal expectations to foster more authentic self-expression.

As we continue to explore these societal norms, we pave the way for more inclusive and realistic expectations that celebrate diversity in women's ambitions and contributions, fostering a society that values each woman for her unique strengths and capabilities.

Influence of Gender Stereotypes

Navigating the landscape of gender stereotypes and societal expectations reveals a complex tapestry that significantly influences women's self-perception and professional lives. These societal norms not only delineate what women can or should be but also subtly erode their confidence, especially in traditionally male-dominated fields. As we delve deeper into how these stereotypes shape feelings of self-doubt among women, it's crucial to explore the pervasive roles of media and the diverse cultural contexts that can either amplify or mitigate these effects.

The Pervasive Impact of Gender Stereotypes

Gender stereotypes are ingrained from an early age and are perpetuated through cultural norms, influencing how women view their roles in both the private and public spheres. These stereotypes often paint a picture of women as less capable of handling leadership roles or technical tasks, which can insidiously affect women's self-assessment of their abilities. For example, in the corporate world, these preconceived notions can lead to fewer women assuming high-level positions, not necessarily because they are less qualified, but because they are perceived as such, both by others and themselves. This misperception is often internalized, leading many women to feel like impostors in their roles—doubting their accomplishments and fearing that they will be exposed as frauds.

The effects of these stereotypes are not just confined to professional settings. In academia, women pursuing degrees in STEM fields may find themselves questioning their intellectual abilities more than their male counterparts, influenced by societal cues that suggest these areas are "not for women." This doubt can diminish their participation and achievement, creating a feedback loop that reinforces the stereotype for the next generation of young women.

Media's Role in Shaping Self-Perception

Media and popular culture play a critical role in framing societal expectations and can either challenge or reinforce harmful stereotypes. Often, media portrayal of women emphasizes physical attractiveness over intellectual contributions, or depicts women in supportive or subordinate roles. These portrayals can set unrealistic standards for success and beauty, which place immense pressure on women to conform to these narrow ideals.

The influence of media extends into how accomplishments are recognized and celebrated. When stories of successful women are shared, they are often accompanied by qualifiers related to their roles as mothers or wives, subtly suggesting that their professional achievements are not enough to define their worth. This skewed representation contributes to a cultural narrative that women's value is contingent upon how well they balance professional success with traditional feminine roles, perpetuating a cycle of doubt about their primary professional capabilities.

Cultural Diversity and Its Impact

The experience and impact of these stereotypes are not uniform but vary greatly across different cultural backgrounds. In some cultures, the community's collective success might overshadow individual achievements, which can diminish the visibility of women's contributions. In contrast, in individualistic societies, where personal success is highly celebrated, the pressure on women to excel and prove themselves can be overwhelming, exacerbating feelings of inadequacy and impostor-like doubts.

Cultural attitudes toward discussing personal doubts and mental health issues can significantly affect how women deal with these feelings. In societies where mental health is openly discussed, women might find more support and resources to overcome their doubts. However, in cultures where such discussions are taboo, women may struggle in silence without the communal or professional support that could help alleviate their feelings of impostorism.

Synthesizing Insights for Change

To effectively address and mitigate the impact of gender stereotypes and societal expectations, a multifaceted approach is necessary. This approach involves promoting media literacy to recognize and challenge unhelpful stereotypes, advocating for more diverse and empowering representations of women, and fostering environments—both professional and academic—that support and celebrate women's achievements without reservation or qualification.

Education plays a pivotal role in this change. By integrating discussions about gender stereotypes and their effects into educational curriculums, we can equip the next generation with the awareness and tools to challenge these outdated norms. Additionally, mentorship programs that connect young women with successful female role models can provide both inspiration and practical guidance, helping to bridge the gap between aspiration and reality.

This comprehensive exploration not only aims to highlight the challenges women face due to entrenched societal norms, but also outlines pathways for empowerment and change. As we continue to challenge these norms, we pave the way for a society that values and respects women's diverse experiences and talents, ultimately fostering a more inclusive and equitable world.

Challenging Societal Expectations

Women, often bound by outdated expectations, find themselves at a crossroads where conforming no longer serves their growth or potential. Here, we delve into strategies for redefining these norms, supplemented by inspiring case studies of women who have paved their own paths, and discuss how promoting inclusivity can reshape societal norms for the better.

Redefining Norms

To challenge and redefine societal expectations, women can employ several strategies that not only question the status quo but also encourage broader acceptance of diverse capabilities and roles. One effective approach is advocacy within professional and social communities. By voicing concerns and pushing for policy changes that support flexible work arrangements, parental leave, and equal pay, women can influence the structural aspects of professional environments that often perpetuate traditional roles.

Education also plays a critical role. Conducting workshops and seminars that highlight the discrepancies between men and women in various fields can enlighten others about the implicit biases that continue to hinder women's progress. Additionally, creating platforms where women can share their experiences and strategies for overcoming barriers can foster a sense of community and collective action.

The power of personal stories cannot be overstated. For instance, consider the story of Malala Yousafzai, who defied Taliban edicts against girls' education in Pakistan to become a global advocate for women's rights to education (Blumberg, 2023). Her courage and determination to pursue education despite life-threatening opposition have inspired countless young women around the world to stand up for their rights.

Another example is Sheryl Sandberg, whose career as the COO of Facebook and her book, *Lean In*, have sparked international discussions about women's roles in business and the challenges they face in leadership positions (*Sheryl Sandberg*, 2024). Her advocacy for women leaning into their careers and challenging the corporate world's gender expectations has ignited a movement encouraging women to aspire to and occupy leadership roles.

Promoting Inclusivity and Acceptance

Enhancing inclusivity starts with recognizing the diverse experiences of women from different backgrounds and respecting the unique challenges they face. Implementing diversity and inclusion training programs in workplaces can educate individuals about the importance of inclusivity and the negative impacts of stereotyping and discrimination.

Additionally, promoting policies that accommodate a variety of life choices can help institutionalize inclusivity. For example, recognizing non-traditional family structures, providing support for single parents, or accommodating different cultural practices within workplaces and educational institutions can create environments where diverse identities and experiences are respected and valued.

Empowering New Normatives

By advocating for changes that recognize and celebrate diversity, challenging outdated norms, and providing platforms for visibility and change, we not only empower individual women but also shift societal perceptions on a larger scale. This shift is crucial for creating a world where women's potential is not limited by preconceived notions of what they can or should be.

As we forge ahead, let's carry the stories of those who have blazed trails, the strategies that have proven effective, and the goal of a more inclusive society as our guides. This journey is not just about challenging norms but about transforming them to empower all women to define their paths and narratives in the broad tapestry of society.

Building Resilience Against External Pressures

In the journey toward systemic change and personal empowerment, building resilience against external pressures is not just beneficial—it's essential. As women, the societal expectations and stereotypes we navigate can often feel like invisible barriers to our progress. By understanding how to bolster our mental and emotional defenses, we can better confront these challenges and pave the way for not only personal growth but also broader societal transformation.

Cultivating Resilience Through Artistic Expression

One powerful yet often overlooked strategy for building psychological resilience is through artistic expression. Engaging in the arts—whether painting, writing, music, or drama—provides a unique conduit for processing complex emotions and experiences, allowing us to externalize what we may struggle to verbalize. Here's how you can integrate artistic expression into your resilience-building practices:

- **Art as a reflective practice:**
    - **Personal art projects:** Start a personal art project that reflects your experiences with societal pressures. This could be a series of paintings, a blog, or even a musical composition. The key is to choose a medium that resonates with you, providing an outlet for creative expression and introspection.

By incorporating artistic expression into your resilience strategy, you tap into a profound source of personal power and community connection. Art transcends language and cultural barriers, offering a universal language that can advocate for change and inspire strength. Through this creative outlet, you not only fortify your own psychological resilience but also contribute to a cultural shift that values and understands the depth of women's experiences in facing societal pressures.

This approach to resilience through art is not merely about creating; it's about transforming the narrative from one of vulnerability to one of empowerment. As we harness our creative energies, we redefine our interactions with the world around us, turning societal pressures into opportunities for growth and expression. This chapter not only guides you in developing personal resilience but also empowers you to contribute actively to societal change, ensuring that your voice, and the voices of women everywhere, are heard, valued, and celebrated.

Empowerment and Community Support

In a world where societal pressures often dictate the trajectories of women's lives, fostering empowerment and community support is not merely beneficial—it's imperative. This narrative is about more than personal growth; it's about collectively challenging the restrictive norms that govern our professional and personal spheres. Through the development of supportive environments, we not only aid individual women in overcoming barriers but also set the stage for widespread societal change.

Creating Transformative Environments

Supportive environments do more than provide a backdrop for growth; they catalyze it. These spaces—whether they're professional networks, social groups, or online platforms—allow for the exchange of ideas, experiences, and strategies that empower women to navigate and reshape their worlds. Mentorship programs, for instance, play a crucial role by pairing emerging leaders with seasoned professionals. These relationships are more than hierarchical connections; they are reciprocal partnerships where both mentors and mentees gain new insights and grow. Such environments encourage resilience and innovation, allowing women to test and redefine their roles in safe, supportive settings.

Addressing Mental Health Within Societal Frameworks

The dual challenge of meeting professional demands while conforming to societal expectations can severely impact mental health, leading to stress, anxiety, and burnout. Addressing this requires more than acknowledgment—it necessitates actionable strategies. Integrating mental health support into the workplace through wellness programs can provide critical resources for managing stress and promoting work-life balance. Additionally, community support groups offer invaluable spaces for women to share their struggles and successes, significantly reducing feelings of isolation.

These groups and programs should not only offer support but also actively work toward dismantling the stigmas associated with seeking help. By normalizing conversations about mental health and providing a platform for these discussions, we can create a more understanding and empathetic community.

Inspiration From the Frontlines of Change

The power of personal stories in driving change cannot be overstated. These narratives do not just inspire—they mobilize and empower. Consider the story of a woman who broke traditional barriers by entering a male-dominated field. Her journey, filled with challenges and triumphs, not only showcases her resilience but also serves as a blueprint for others. Similarly, the story of a community leader who advocated for family-friendly work policies illustrates how individual efforts can lead to substantial societal shifts. These stories highlight the importance of personal agency and the impact of supportive networks in overcoming societal challenges.

These narratives also reinforce the value of visibility and representation. By sharing their stories, women not only pave the way for others but also contribute to a broader narrative that challenges and reshapes societal expectations. These stories foster a culture of success and empowerment that transcends individual achievements, promoting a collective rise.

Cultivating a Culture of Empowerment

As we move forward, the lessons learned from these empowerment strategies and stories are not just about overcoming challenges but about redefining the parameters of success and fulfillment. The next step is to leverage this foundation to not only continue supporting individual women but also to challenge and transform the societal norms that create these pressures. By promoting a culture that values diverse narratives and encourages open dialogue about challenges and successes, we can begin to dismantle the outdated frameworks that limit women's potential.

This chapter is not merely a collection of strategies but a call to action—a directive to forge supportive communities, prioritize mental health, and celebrate the diverse stories of resilience and success. As we transition to the next chapter, we build on this groundwork, focusing on internal barriers that women often face and exploring how personal values and beliefs can influence and enhance their journey toward empowerment and self-acceptance. This exploration is crucial for anyone seeking to not just navigate but actively reshape the societal landscapes that impact us all.

Chapter 5:

Breaking Barriers: Dismantling Self-Imposed Limitations

Standing at the threshold of our potential, we often find that the most formidable barriers to success and personal fulfillment originate from within ourselves. These self-imposed limitations, subtly woven into our everyday thoughts and actions, might not always be visible, but they significantly shape our experiences and achievements. They whisper doubts when opportunities arise and craft ceilings that feel too solid to break. But what if we could identify these barriers, understand their origins, and dismantle them piece by piece?

Throughout this chapter, remember that the goal is not to suppress our fears or insecurities but to confront them bravely and with a clear mindset as we move forward. It's about building a resilient self that can navigate challenges with confidence and grace. The path to breaking these barriers is paved with persistence, insight, and the unwavering belief that we are capable of more than we might currently imagine. Let's take the first step together, challenging the limitations we've set for ourselves and embracing a future where we are defined not by our doubts but by our determination to overcome them.

Techniques to Identify and Challenge Negative Self-Talk

Addressing negative self-talk is crucial when tackling self-imposed limitations. This internal dialogue can sabotage our best intentions and diminish our confidence, often without us even realizing its impact. By employing specific techniques, such as cognitive restructuring exercises, affirmations, and mindset shifts, we can begin to transform these destructive patterns into empowering beliefs that support our growth and success.

Cognitive Restructuring Exercises

Cognitive restructuring is a powerful tool in cognitive-behavioral therapy that involves identifying and challenging irrational or maladaptive thoughts. The process begins by becoming acutely aware of the negative thoughts that frequently invade our minds. Once these thoughts are identified, the challenge is to test their validity and reshape them into more positive, constructive thoughts. For instance, if you often think, *I can never do this right*, you might reframe it to, *I am capable of learning and improving with practice*. Such exercises not only diminish the power of negative thinking but also reinforce your ability to approach situations with a healthier, more optimistic mindset.

Affirmations and Mindset Shifts

Affirmations are positive statements that can counteract the negativity that often infiltrates our thoughts, particularly when we face new challenges or setbacks. By regularly practicing affirmations, such as "I am competent, smart, and capable," we can begin to internalize these qualities, slowly shifting our mindset from one of self-doubt to one of self-assurance and resilience. The key is consistency; affirmations are most effective when integrated into daily routines, allowing them to seep into our subconscious and gradually alter our fundamental self-beliefs.

Recognizing and Reframing Self-Limiting Beliefs

The journey toward overcoming self-limiting beliefs is not just about changing how we talk to ourselves; it's also about understanding the behaviors these beliefs spawn. Often, what we dismiss as habitual caution or realistic self-assessment may actually be behaviors stemming from deeper, unexamined beliefs that we are not good enough or that success is beyond our reach. Recognizing these patterns is the first step in dismantling them.

For example, if you habitually avoid taking on challenging projects for fear of failure, this behavior likely stems from a deep-seated belief in your own inadequacy. By acknowledging this cycle, you can begin to confront these fears directly, challenging yourself to take on just one such project with the support of a mentor or peer. Each small success in these ventures provides real-life evidence against the limiting belief, helping to dismantle it over time.

By combining these techniques—cognitive restructuring to tackle the thoughts, affirmations to reshape the dialogue, and behavioral insights to understand the actions—we create a robust framework for personal growth. Curious about how these techniques can be applied day-to-day? Our companion journal provides detailed exercises and practical guides to help you integrate these transformative strategies into your everyday life.

This approach not only addresses the symptoms of self-doubt but strikes at the root, enabling a profound and lasting transformation that empowers us to reach beyond what we once saw as our limits.

Strategies for Overcoming Perfectionistic Tendencies

As we delve deeper into the realm of self-imposed barriers, one of the most pervasive issues I encounter is perfectionism. This drive to make everything flawless can often lead to significant stress and hinder your progress by setting unattainable standards. Understanding how to recognize and temper this tendency is crucial for your personal and professional development.

Recognizing and Reducing Perfectionism

First, it's important for you to recognize the signs of perfectionism in your behavior. Do you find yourself obsessing over minor details that others may not notice? Are you often dissatisfied with your work even when it receives praise from others? These can be indicators that your standards might be set too high, leading to unnecessary stress and burnout.

To reduce perfectionism, start by setting more realistic goals. This doesn't mean lowering your standards but understanding what is achievable within a given timeframe and accepting that sometimes "good enough" is sufficient for the task at hand. Another effective strategy is to practice time-limited activities. Give yourself a set amount of time for a task, and when that time is up, move on. This helps to combat the urge to tweak and refine endlessly.

I've had the privilege of learning from individuals who have successfully navigated their perfectionistic tendencies to foster healthier, more productive behaviors. For example, Sarah, a graphic designer, used to spend extra hours on projects, tweaking minor details invisible to others. Through coaching, she learned to set clear objectives for her projects and define what success looked like before starting. This shift allowed her to focus on meeting these goals rather than getting lost in the details. Sarah's story is a powerful reminder that by redefining our approach to work, we can transform our perfectionistic impulses into a drive for excellence that doesn't compromise our well-being.

The Impact of Perfectionism on Decision-Making and Self-Sabotage

Perfectionism doesn't just affect how you complete tasks; it can also influence your decision-making processes, leading to procrastination and self-sabotage. The fear of making the wrong decision can paralyze you, preventing you from taking steps that could lead to significant opportunities (Liu et al., 2022).

To break free from these cycles, it's helpful to develop a decision-making framework. Start by identifying the decision to be made, gather necessary information, and set a deadline for making the decision. By structuring your decision-making process, you can reduce the anxiety associated with it and avoid the procrastination that often comes with the desire to make the "perfect" choice.

Tackling perfectionism is not about compromising your desire to achieve but about channeling this energy in ways that boost your efficiency and well-being. By recognizing and adjusting your perfectionistic tendencies, you can avoid the stress and stalled progress that often accompany them. If you're seeking to develop healthier, more balanced approaches to your work and life, our companion journal provides a wealth of resources and tools designed to help you manage and mitigate perfectionism effectively.

As we continue to explore these themes, remember that the journey to overcome self-imposed limitations is continuous. Each step you take builds upon the last, creating a foundation of resilience and self-awareness that supports all areas of your life.

The Role of Fear and Past Experiences

In our exploration of self-imposed barriers, it's crucial to understand the profound impact that fear and past experiences have on shaping our present behaviors and beliefs. These deep-seated fears don't just appear out of nowhere; they are often rooted in early life experiences that have left a lasting imprint. By addressing these fears directly, you can begin to dismantle the limiting beliefs they sustain and open the door to a more empowered version of yourself.

Understanding the Impact of Fear

Fear is a powerful motivator that can either spur us to action or paralyze us. In the context of self-limitation, fear often manifests as a deterrent to stepping out of comfort zones, trying new things, or pursuing ambitions. It can make you doubt your capabilities and second-guess your decisions, trapping you in a cycle of what-ifs and not-good-enoughs.

To combat these fears, it's important to first acknowledge them. I encourage you to write down your fears as they relate to your personal and professional life. Seeing them on paper can make them less daunting and more manageable. From there, challenge these fears by asking yourself what evidence exists to support or refute them. This exercise, known as fear-setting, can be incredibly liberating as it helps put into perspective what is truly at risk and what is merely a construct of internalized anxiety.

Tools for Empowerment: Challenging Deep-Seated Fears

One effective tool for challenging deep-seated fears is visualization. Imagine yourself successfully navigating a situation you fear, focusing on the feelings of accomplishment and confidence that come with overcoming obstacles. Regularly practicing this visualization can gradually diminish the power that fear holds over you and reinforce a positive self-image.

Another powerful approach is to gradually expose yourself to the things you fear in a controlled, manageable way. This method, known as systematic desensitization, helps reduce the anxiety associated with specific fears and can be very effective for fears related to performance, such as public speaking or taking on leadership roles.

The Influence of Childhood Experiences

Many of our fears and limiting beliefs originate in childhood, a time when we are most impressionable. Negative experiences during these formative years, such as criticism from authority figures or traumatic events, can profoundly influence how we view ourselves and our abilities.

Addressing these childhood experiences is essential for healing and growth. Techniques such as narrative therapy can be useful here; this involves rewriting the narratives of your past experiences to highlight resilience and empowerment instead of fear and victimhood. Professional therapy can provide a safe space to explore these past traumas with the guidance of someone who can help you process and overcome them.

Strategies for Releasing Past Traumas

Releasing the hold that past traumas have on you often requires a multifaceted approach. Apart from therapy, practices like breath work, meditation, and journaling can help you stay present and engage with your emotions in a non-judgmental way. These practices encourage a form of self-compassion that is crucial for healing.

Joining support groups where you can share your experiences and learn from others who have faced similar challenges can reinforce the understanding that you are not alone in this journey. The shared experiences and collective wisdom found in these groups can be incredibly validating and empowering.

As you work through these strategies and start confronting the fears and past experiences that shape your limiting beliefs, remember that progress is a gradual process. Each step you take is a move toward a more empowered and fearless version of yourself, capable of transcending the barriers that once seemed insurmountable.

The Power of Positive Affirmations and Self-Compassion

In our journey toward breaking free from self-imposed limitations, it's essential to cultivate tools that can directly combat the roots of negativity within us. Positive affirmations and the practice of self-compassion are not just soothing salves for the soul; they are powerful techniques that can radically transform how you see yourself and interact with the world.

Cultivating a Positive Self-Image With Affirmations

Positive affirmations are simple yet powerful statements that, when spoken repeatedly, can help reinforce a positive self-image and challenge the pervasive effects of negative self-talk. These affirmations work by slowly reshaping your subconscious beliefs, aligning them more closely with your conscious aspirations and goals.

To begin integrating affirmations into your life, start by identifying the areas where you feel most vulnerable or doubtful. For instance, if you often feel inadequate in your professional skills, you might adopt an affirmation like, "I am competent and skilled in my work." Repeating this affirmation daily, especially during moments of doubt, can gradually replace the negative narrative with a more empowering one.

Developing Personalized Plans to Overcome Limiting Beliefs

While affirmations and self-compassion are powerful, their effectiveness increases significantly when used as part of a broader, personalized plan to tackle specific limiting beliefs. To create this plan, follow these steps:

1. **Identify limiting beliefs:** Write down specific beliefs that hold you back. Be as detailed as possible in describing how they affect your behavior and emotions.

2. **Challenge each belief:** For each belief, write a counter statement that challenges its validity. Use evidence from your experiences that disproves the negative belief.

3. **Set small, manageable goals:** Break down the process of overcoming each belief into small, achievable goals. This could involve practicing a specific affirmation, engaging in a particular self-compassion exercise, or taking a small risk that contradicts the limiting belief.

4. **Review and adjust:** Regularly review your progress and adjust your approach as needed. This might mean refining your affirmations, finding new ways to integrate self-compassion, or setting different goals.

As you work through these strategies, you'll find that your internal dialogue begins to change. The voice of self-doubt becomes quieter, and in its place, a more supportive and compassionate voice emerges. This new voice is your true ally, one that champions your cause and supports your journey toward fulfilling your potential. As we continue to explore and apply these transformative practices, remember that each step forward is a step away from the limitations of yesterday and a move toward a more empowered tomorrow.

Fostering Lifelong Growth and Community Support

In our pursuit of personal excellence and dismantling self-imposed limitations, it's essential to embrace a mindset of continuous growth and resilience. This approach isn't just about overcoming hurdles; it's about seeing each day as a new opportunity to expand beyond our previous boundaries, nurturing habits that promote adaptability and learning.

Consider the power of resilience through stories like Emily's, who conquered a profound fear of public speaking to become a celebrated motivational speaker. Her journey highlights how perceived barriers are often just misperceptions waiting to be dismantled by perseverance and self-belief. Similarly, Johanna's story of career transformation in his late forties reminds us that it's never too late to redefine our paths and pursue new passions, even in fields as challenging as climate change research.

As we learn from these examples, we must also commit to supporting others on their paths to growth. Offering a hand might mean sharing encouraging words, engaging in mentoring, or creating supportive networks where individuals can safely share their struggles and victories. We can organize workshops or discussion groups focused on resilience and setting realistic goals, enhancing not just individual journeys but also strengthening our community's collective resilience.

This continuous cycle of personal development and community support doesn't just break down our own barriers—it also lays down a foundation for collective empowerment and progress. By recognizing and celebrating each step forward, we create an environment where growth is not just an individual achievement but a shared victory.

As we close this chapter on overcoming self-imposed barriers and fostering community support, let us carry forward the lessons of resilience and empowerment. The journey of self-improvement is ongoing, filled with opportunities to both teach and learn, to give and receive support. The next chapter will shift our focus from internal efforts to external recognitions, celebrating the milestones we've achieved and setting the stage for future successes. This recognition is crucial, not just for personal validation but also as a beacon for others to follow, demonstrating the tangible rewards of dedication and self-belief.

Chapter 6:

Celebrating You: Illuminating Your Achievements

Every step forward in our lives deserves recognition, yet too often, we overlook our own successes, hurrying onto the next challenge without a moment's reflection. In a world that often rushes us from one goal to the next, taking the time to pause and celebrate your successes is not just a reward—it's an essential practice for sustainable growth and self-recognition.

Celebrating your successes does more than just boost your morale; it reinforces your identity as a capable individual. It combats the often subtle narrative that undermines your confidence and shadows your achievements with doubt.

By the end of this chapter, you'll have not only a deeper appreciation for what you've accomplished but also the tools to keep that appreciation glowing brightly, guiding you forward as you continue to set and reach new goals. Let's embark on this journey of celebration and self-discovery, ensuring that every step forward is acknowledged and every success, no matter how small, is celebrated.

Building a Portfolio of Achievements

Creating a dynamic portfolio of your achievements is an essential step toward recognizing your progress and understanding the unique skills you bring to your endeavors. This portfolio not only serves as a testament to your successes but also acts as a reflective tool that helps solidify your confidence and competencies.

Documenting Your Successes Strategically

Start by laying out your achievements in chronological order. Include everything from significant milestones to smaller yet meaningful victories. For each entry, go beyond simply stating the outcome. Detail the specific challenges you faced and the strategies you employed to address them. This method not only shows your problem-solving abilities but also your capacity to navigate obstacles effectively.

Next, identify and list the skills that each achievement showcases. Whether these are technical skills or soft skills like leadership and communication, noting them explicitly ties your successes to tangible competencies. Additionally, reflect on the lessons each experience taught you. Integrating these insights into your portfolio will increase your awareness of your own abilities.

Valuing Your Skills and Contributions

Conduct a regular skills audit to evaluate and appreciate the range of capabilities you possess. This practice helps you recognize your strengths and identify areas for growth, reinforcing your self-esteem. Also, gathering feedback from peers and mentors can provide external validation of your abilities and help you see your contributions through a new lens.

Organize your portfolio to highlight achievements that underscore key skills. If creativity is one of your strengths, for example, prominently feature projects where innovative thinking was crucial. This not only personalizes your portfolio but also makes it a compelling narrative of your professional journey.

Enhancing Self-Perception With Your Portfolio

Utilize your achievements portfolio as a tool to counteract feelings of self-doubt. Regularly reviewing your portfolio, especially during times of uncertainty or before critical career events like interviews or evaluations, can reaffirm your capabilities and accomplishments. This practice serves as a powerful reminder of your qualifications and the positive impact of your work.

Additionally, sharing your portfolio with your network can further reinforce your professional identity and boost your confidence. Receiving acknowledgment and praise from peers can be incredibly affirming and serve as a motivator for future endeavors.

This living document encourages a proactive approach to career and personal development, setting the stage for the next section, where we delve deeper into the strategies for reframing accomplishments in a positive light. By seamlessly connecting your documented achievements with forward-thinking strategies, we pave the way for continued growth and self-improvement.

Tools for Reframing Accomplishments

As we continue to build upon the foundation of recognizing and documenting our achievements, it's equally important to consider how we perceive and frame these accomplishments. Reframing them positively can profoundly impact our self-esteem and motivation. Here, I'll guide you through techniques to view your successes in a new light and introduce methods to visually represent your achievements, enhancing their perceived value and impact.

Positive Reframing Techniques

Positive reframing involves altering your perspective on past events to emphasize the positive aspects and the value they've added to your growth. This technique is particularly useful when you feel that certain accomplishments aren't "big enough" or don't measure up to external standards. To practice this, start by listing your achievements, focusing on the skills you developed and the challenges you overcame.

Ask yourself questions like, "What did I learn from this experience?" or, "How did this make me better at what I do?" These questions help shift the focus from what was lacking to what was gained. For instance, even if a project didn't succeed as expected, focusing on the project management skills you honed during the process adds a positive spin and recognizes personal growth.

Visual Representation of Successes

Creating visual representations of your achievements can make them more tangible and easier to appreciate. Techniques like infographics, achievement timelines, or even a simple visual board can serve as powerful reminders of your journey and successes.

For example, an infographic could highlight key milestones in your career, supplemented by icons or statistics that quantify your impact, such as revenue generated, projects led, or people trained. These visuals serve not just as a personal reminder but can also be used in professional settings, such as during performance reviews or networking events, to quickly convey your capabilities and achievements.

Drawing on Effective Reframing Examples

The website Open Space Clinic offers excellent insights on how to overcome doubts and start embracing your successes by reframing accomplishments. According to their advice, an effective way to reframe might involve changing your narrative from "I just got lucky" to "I was well-prepared and my efforts paid off," which acknowledges your role in your successes.

By incorporating these techniques and adopting a new mindset about your accomplishments, you reinforce your sense of agency and impact in your career and personal life. This approach not only boosts your confidence but also prepares you to tackle future challenges with a stronger outlook.

Navigating Self-Doubt in Career Achievements

As you progress through your career, understanding the importance of both external recognition and internal validation is essential for bolstering self-confidence and effectively managing self-doubt. Recognizing your achievements and the skills that led to them isn't just about feeling good—it's about building a foundation of confidence that sustains your growth and aspirations.

The Role of Acknowledgment and Validation

Gaining acknowledgment from peers and superiors can have a profound impact on how you view your capabilities. This external validation confirms that your contributions are valuable and impactful, which can be a significant boost to your confidence. However, it's crucial to balance this with self-validation. Regularly acknowledging your own efforts and successes helps you develop resilience against external fluctuations in recognition and feedback.

To foster this balance, make it a habit to reflect on your weekly or monthly achievements. Write them down and review them regularly to internalize your progress and contributions. This practice of self-recognition nurtures a steady sense of self-worth that is less dependent on external validation.

Learning From Inspirational Case Studies

Inspirational stories, like those highlighted by Miles (n.d.), showcase the transformative power of embracing achievements and overcoming doubts by tapping into one's unique strengths. These narratives often reveal how individuals like Michelle Obama and Sheryl Sandberg overcame their doubts by focusing on their unique contributions, even when they felt overshadowed by perceived inadequacies. For instance, a female founder doubted her abilities due to her non-technical background, yet she learned to harness her strengths in visionary leadership and strategic planning to excel.

These stories serve as powerful reminders of the value of your unique skills and perspectives, particularly when external judgments may cloud your self-perception. Each story not only inspires but also offers practical strategies for women to navigate their own doubts and build confidence in their abilities.

Setting Realistic Expectations

Setting realistic goals is another key strategy for combating career-related self-doubt. Unachievable goals can lead to frustration and self-recrimination, which only feed into a cycle of doubt. Instead, aim to set clear, measurable, and attainable goals that build on your existing skills and push you to grow without setting you up for failure.

Break your larger goals into smaller, actionable steps that allow you to celebrate small wins regularly. This approach not only keeps you motivated but also creates a positive feedback loop where each success builds upon the last. Regularly reassess and adjust these goals to ensure they remain aligned with your professional growth and personal aspirations.

Continue to build on these practices, remembering that each step forward, recognized and appreciated, strengthens your journey toward a fulfilling and successful career. Our companion journal extends this discussion, offering strategies to balance external recognition with internal validation, and provides tools to fortify your self-belief in competitive environments.

Navigating Doubts in Personal Relationships

In our personal relationships, just as in our professional lives, we often face doubts about our worthiness and the validity of our achievements. These doubts can lead us to undervalue the successes we've worked hard to attain. Understanding how to navigate these feelings in our personal interactions is crucial for maintaining healthy, supportive relationships that encourage growth and confidence.

It's common to question our achievements and sometimes feel like we haven't truly earned our successes. These doubts can be particularly pronounced when we compare ourselves to friends, family, or partners who might have different accomplishments or life paths. Recognizing this tendency is the first step toward addressing it. Acknowledge that these feelings are normal, but they don't have to define your self-worth or the authenticity of your achievements.

Building a Supportive Community

One of the most effective ways to combat self-doubt is to cultivate an inner circle that actively celebrates each other's successes. This support network should include people who understand and share your values and aspirations. Here are a few strategies to foster such a community:

- **Encourage open dialogue:** Create spaces where friends and family can discuss their achievements and challenges openly. This promotes a culture of transparency and mutual support.

- **Celebrate small wins:** Make it a practice within your circle to celebrate small victories as well as big ones. Whether it's a job promotion, mastering a new skill, or simply overcoming a personal challenge, recognizing these moments can boost everyone's confidence.

- **Offer genuine praise:** When someone in your community achieves something, offer sincere praise and recognition. Highlight specific aspects of their achievement to show that you appreciate their effort and success.

Understanding and addressing how we perceive and share our achievements can significantly influence our personal relationships. Often, we might inadvertently diminish our own accomplishments, which can affect how we interact and connect with those closest to us. Recognizing and breaking this cycle of doubt within personal contexts is crucial for fostering healthier, more supportive interactions.

Creating an environment where successes are openly celebrated can profoundly impact our self-esteem and the dynamics of our personal relationships. For example, incorporating practices like regular family meetings where everyone shares recent achievements or organizing gatherings with friends to celebrate professional milestones can cultivate a culture of recognition and encouragement. These practices help reinforce personal value and build a supportive community that celebrates each individual's success.

As we conclude this chapter, it's clear that recognizing and celebrating achievements is fundamental not just for personal validation but for nurturing our growth and relationships. These practices not only enhance our sense of self-worth but also encourage us to live a life marked by acknowledgment and appreciation of our efforts and successes.

Looking ahead, we will explore how extending compassion to ourselves can transform our approach to life's challenges and enrich our interactions with others. By learning to treat ourselves with kindness, we can better navigate the complexities of our emotions and relationships, fostering a more compassionate and fulfilling life.

Chapter 7:

Cultivating Self-Compassion

Self-compassion is an essential, yet often overlooked, component of emotional well-being. It involves treating yourself with the same kindness and understanding you would offer a good friend during times of difficulty. Unlike self-esteem, which is contingent on success and often involves comparisons with others, self-compassion is about being kind to yourself regardless of your achievements or failures. This chapter will guide you through the foundational principles of self-compassion, highlighting its significance and the distinct elements that comprise it.

At its core, self-compassion is the practice of being gentle and empathetic toward oneself in instances of perceived inadequacy, failure, or general suffering. This approach is crucial because it allows for a kinder and more realistic self-view, fostering resilience against life's inevitable setbacks. Self-compassion provides a stable sense of self-worth that does not depend on external factors. This stability is vital for maintaining mental health and emotional well-being, as it helps to buffer against anxiety, depression, and the stress of unrealistic self-expectations.

Core Components of Self-Compassion

Self-compassion can be divided into three interconnected components, each contributing to a healthier, more compassionate self-relationship:

1. **Self-kindness vs. self-judgment:** This component involves being warm toward oneself when encountering pain and personal shortcomings rather than ignoring them or hurting oneself with self-criticism. Self-kindness recognizes that imperfection is part of the human experience and offers comfort to oneself, much like we would to a friend in distress.

2. **Common humanity vs. isolation:** Common humanity is the recognition that suffering and personal failure are universal experiences—not something that happens to you alone. This perspective helps reduce feelings of loneliness and isolation by reinforcing the interconnectedness of our human experience.

3. **Mindfulness vs. over-identification:** Mindfulness in self-compassion involves a balanced approach to negative emotions so that feelings are neither suppressed nor exaggerated. This balanced awareness is crucial in relating to our experiences objectively and empathetically, allowing us to acknowledge our pains and disappointments without allowing them to define us.

By integrating these components into your daily life, you can begin to shift the way you relate to yourself. Practicing self-kindness, recognizing our shared human experience, and maintaining a balanced perspective on our emotions equip us to handle life's challenges with greater ease and confidence. As we cultivate self-compassion, we not only improve our relationship with ourselves but also enhance our interactions with others, promoting a more empathetic and understanding approach to all our relationships.

As we continue this exploration, you'll learn practical strategies to deepen your understanding of self-compassion and integrate it into every aspect of your life, fostering an enduring sense of peace and self-acceptance. This foundation of self-compassion not only enriches your personal life but also sets the stage for discussing how to apply these principles to overcome guilt and shame, which we will explore next.

Practical Exercises for Cultivating Self-Compassion

Cultivating self-compassion is an active practice that involves engaging with specific exercises that can retrain your mind and heart to respond more kindly to your own experiences of suffering or perceived inadequacies. Here, I'll introduce you to effective mindfulness techniques and guided meditations that are particularly beneficial for fostering a compassionate attitude toward yourself.

Mindfulness Techniques

Mindfulness is a foundational tool for developing self-compassion. It helps you become more aware of the present moment and teaches you to observe your thoughts and feelings without judgment. Incorporate this easy mindfulness exercise into your everyday schedule:

- **Mindful breathing:** This exercise involves focusing your attention on your breath, the inhalation and exhalation, as a way to anchor yourself in the present moment. Whenever you find yourself overwhelmed by negative thoughts or feelings, take a few minutes to breathe deeply. Count to four as you inhale, hold for a count of four, and exhale for a count of four. This practice can help center your thoughts and reduce reactivity to self-critical thoughts.

Guided Meditations

Guided meditations can be particularly helpful for those who are new to meditation or find it challenging to focus. These meditations use soothing narratives or specific instructions to lead you through a meditation practice focused on cultivating self-compassion.

- **Loving-kindness meditation:** This meditation involves silently repeating phrases that wish well-being, happiness, and ease to yourself and others. Start with yourself, then gradually extend that kindness outward to friends, family, acquaintances, and eventually, to all beings. Some example phrases include, "May I be happy," "May I be healthy," "May I be safe," and "May I live with ease."

By practicing these techniques, you begin to develop a more compassionate inner voice—one that supports and cares for you in the same way you would support a loved one. Integrating these practices into your daily life not only helps reduce self-criticism and isolation but also enhances your overall emotional resilience, making it easier to navigate life's ups and downs with grace and kindness. These tools are tailored to help you build a consistent practice.

As you become more comfortable with these practices, you'll likely discover an enhanced ability to extend compassion not just to yourself but to others as well, enriching your personal and professional relationships.

Addressing Emotional Barriers: Guilt, Shame, and Self-Doubt

Guilt and shame are intense emotions that can erode our self-compassion and magnify feelings of inadequacy, often manifesting as imposter syndrome. Understanding and differentiating these emotions and developing strategies to mitigate their effects are crucial steps in cultivating a more compassionate and forgiving relationship with yourself.

Understanding Guilt and Shame

Guilt is an emotion tied to a specific action or behavior, where you might feel regret for something you've done wrong, like missing a deadline. It can be a motivating force, pushing you to make amends and learn from mistakes. In contrast, shame is deeper and more destructive—it affects how you see your entire self, making you feel fundamentally flawed or unworthy.

The first step in transforming these feelings is to recognize them without judgment through mindfulness. This acknowledgment allows you to start changing how you react to these emotions:

1. **Reframe negative thoughts:** Shift your internal narrative from self-criticism to understanding and kindness. For example, replace thoughts like "I so

stupid" with "I made a mistake, and that's okay; everyone makes mistakes."

2. **Foster a compassionate inner dialogue:** Develop kinder self-talk. Challenge the harsh inner critic by speaking to yourself as you would to a friend in distress.

3. **Embrace forgiveness:** Particularly with guilt, allowing yourself to forgive your own mistakes is vital. Recognize that perfection is unattainable and that errors are part of human growth.

Imposter syndrome—feeling like a fraud despite evident success—often stems from these deeper feelings of shame and self-doubt. Cultivating self-compassion is a powerful antidote:

- **Practice self-compassion regularly:** Engage in daily self-compassion exercises like journaling positive achievements or meditating on loving-kindness to reinforce your intrinsic worth.

- **Recognize common humanity:** Understand that not feeling good enough is a nearly universal experience, which can help lessen the isolation that imposter syndrome often brings.

A powerful example of overcoming these challenges is detailed by Lauren Harlow (2021). She describes how imposter syndrome deeply affected their life and career. They recount the journey of acknowledging their achievements and gradually learning to accept and celebrate their true self without the cloud of self-doubt. Through regular self-compassion practices, they transformed their approach to personal failures and successes, shifting from self-judgment to acceptance and self-appreciation.

By addressing guilt and shame directly and fostering a nurturing inner dialogue, you can build a foundation of self-compassion that supports lasting personal growth and resilience. This journey is about more than just combating negative feelings; it's about embracing a full, compassionate acceptance of yourself, which enriches all aspects of your life. As you continue to practice these techniques, you'll find that you not only become kinder to yourself but also enhance your ability to face life's challenges with confidence and grace.

Cultivating a Mindset of Kindness and Understanding Toward Oneself

In the pursuit of enhanced mental health, the cultivation of a mindset steeped in kindness and understanding toward oneself proves essential. Self-compassion is not only instrumental in building resilience during challenging times but also significantly boosts overall well-being by influencing our daily interactions with ourselves.

Cultivating Resilience Through Self-Compassion

Resilience is the capacity to recover quickly from difficulties, and self-compassion is a fundamental element in nurturing this trait. By approaching ourselves with kindness and acknowledging that suffering is a part of the shared human condition, we navigate life's challenges with greater ease and reduced apprehension. Here are effective strategies to strengthen resilience through self-compassion:

- **Practice mindful acceptance:** Embrace your feelings during tough times without judgment. Engaging in mindfulness allows you to experience your emotions authentically, laying the groundwork for constructive emotional processing.

- **Reframe negative thoughts:** Shift your internal narrative during setbacks to be more nurturing and supportive. Instead of succumbing to self-criticism, encourage yourself as you would a friend, focusing on constructive feedback and compassionate reassurance.

The Crucial Link Between Self-Compassion and Mental Well-Being

Evidence suggests that self-compassion is closely linked to enhanced mental health. It moderates emotional responses to failures and perceived shortcomings, reducing the intensity of negative impacts on our psychological state. This correlation underscores the importance of nurturing a supportive inner dialogue, which is crucial for maintaining long-term emotional health.

Navigating Societal Expectations

Often, societal norms impose unrealistically high standards that can erode self-compassion and self-esteem. By recognizing and understanding these external pressures, you can cultivate a more forgiving viewpoint toward yourself, accepting that it is perfectly acceptable not to fulfill every societal expectation.

Incorporating self-compassion into daily life is a transformative practice that fosters not only personal growth but also enhances our interactions with others. As we become kinder to ourselves, we are naturally more empathetic and patient with those around us, promoting healthier, more supportive relationships.

For those seeking to delve deeper into self-compassion, our companion journal offers a wealth of resources and detailed strategies designed to foster this vital trait. It serves as a guide to nurturing a compassionate inner dialogue, enhancing your capacity to handle life's challenges with grace, and enriching your overall emotional and mental well-being.

Tools for Integrating Self-Compassion Into Daily Routines and Habits

Self-compassion not only improves how you treat yourself but also how you interact with others. By adopting a compassionate approach to personal challenges, you can foster healthier and more supportive relationships. This practice encourages a more empathetic response to conflicts and a greater understanding of others' perspectives, enriching your social interactions and strengthening bonds with friends, family, and colleagues.

Here are three ways to make these tools actionable:

1. **Set self-compassion reminders:** Use phone alerts or sticky notes as cues to engage in positive self-talk or mindfulness throughout your day.

2. **Journal for gratitude and reflection:** Regularly write down what you are grateful for and moments where you practiced self-kindness, reinforcing the positive impacts of self-compassion.

3. **Incorporate mindful exercises:** Dedicate time each day for activities like yoga or meditation that center your thoughts and calm your mind, linking physical well-being with emotional health.

By consistently applying these strategies, you can ensure that self-compassion becomes a cornerstone of your daily routine, fostering a nurturing internal environment and enhancing your interactions with others. For more detailed guidance and additional strategies, refer to our companion journal, which provides step-by-step instructions on implementing these practices effectively.

This approach not only helps overcome personal and professional challenges but also lays a foundation for lasting well-being and success, ensuring you can handle life's stresses with grace and resilience.

Addressing Self-Care Imbalances With Self-Compassion

Navigating feelings of inadequacy, often magnified by what is termed as imposter syndrome, requires a nuanced understanding of how our self-care practices—or the lack thereof—impact our emotional and psychological states. Self-compassion emerges as a pivotal tool in rebalancing our approach to self-care, guiding us away from self-doubt toward a more confident, self-assured persona. This transformative journey involves not just recognizing our emotional hurdles but actively reshaping our internal dialogues from criticism to compassion.

The journey to embracing self-compassion often includes personal battles with guilt and shame, emotions frequently accompanying feelings of fraudulence or imposter syndrome. Consider the story of Emma, a young professional who grappled with crippling self-doubt early in her career. Despite her accomplishments, Emma constantly felt undeserving and feared being exposed as a fraud. By integrating self-compassion practices into her daily routine, Emma began to see herself as worthy and competent, independent of external validation. Her transformation was marked by an increasing ability to forgive her mistakes and celebrate her successes, illustrating the profound impact of self-compassion in overcoming deep-seated insecurities.

In educational and professional environments, cultivating a culture of self-compassion can significantly mitigate feelings of imposter syndrome. Strategies such as incorporating workshops on self-compassion, integrating mindfulness training into curricula, and providing resources for emotional health support are crucial. These initiatives help individuals understand that personal setbacks and feelings of inadequacy are common, shared experiences rather than individual failings. By promoting an understanding of our common humanity, these settings encourage a more empathetic and supportive approach to personal and professional challenges.

Moreover, self-compassion profoundly improves our relationships with others. By treating ourselves with kindness and understanding, we naturally extend the same empathy, patience, and support to those around us. This approach fosters healthier, more supportive relationships both in personal life and at work. Encouraging open discussions about the importance of emotional self-care and demonstrating self-compassion can lead to more authentic and supportive interactions.

Addressing imposter syndrome effectively requires practical tools that encourage self-compassion. Daily self-compassion journals, for instance, allow individuals to reflect on their feelings and respond to negative self-talk with compassionate affirmations. Developing "self-compassion mantras," which can be recited during moments of self-doubt, helps reinforce a compassionate perspective toward oneself. These tools are instrumental in transforming how we perceive and engage with ourselves, shifting from a narrative of inadequacy to one of empowerment.

The role of self-forgiveness and acceptance in combating feelings associated with imposter syndrome cannot be overstated. Writing forgiveness letters to oneself is a powerful exercise in acknowledging past judgments and moving forward with a compassionate outlook. Regular practice of these techniques can cultivate resilience against the harsh internal critic that often drives imposter feelings.

As we continue to explore and implement these strategies, a balanced and compassionate self-view becomes increasingly attainable. This transformation enriches all facets of life, enhancing personal and professional growth and fostering healthier relationships.

This section not only guides you in overcoming imposter syndrome but also enriches your personal and professional life, establishing a robust foundation for enduring self-confidence and emotional well-being.

The Role of Self-Compassion in Fostering Resilience and Emotional Strength

Self-compassion is far more than a mere soothing balm for the soul; it is a foundational strength that enhances resilience and facilitates substantial emotional growth. By learning to treat ourselves with kindness, especially during challenging times, we foster a robustness that improves our ability to handle life's fluctuations with grace and poise.

Empowerment through self-compassion begins by recognizing that kindness to oneself boosts our engagement with life proactively. Daily practices such as setting aside time for self-reflection, speaking to ourselves kindly during difficult moments, and celebrating small victories can significantly enhance our resilience. These practices facilitate a shift from a mindset dominated by self-criticism to one filled with encouragement and support, which promotes growth and proactive engagement with our goals and challenges.

Maintaining a positive self-image through self-compassion involves recognizing our inherent worth, irrespective of external achievements or failures. This approach is crucial for sustaining emotional health and resilience, steering us away from the pitfalls of relying solely on external validation. This can be destabilizing, especially when facing professional setbacks or personal criticisms.

The transformative power of self-compassion is vividly illustrated through the experiences of women who have thrived by embracing this practice. For example, consider Maya, a corporate executive who faced severe burnout and self-doubt. By incorporating self-compassion into her daily routine, she transitioned from near collapse to flourishing both in her career and personal life. This journey underscores the critical role self-compassion plays in recovery and success. Similarly, Ava, a community leader, not only enhanced her well-being through self-kindness but also inspired her team to embrace these practices. Her leadership led to improved group dynamics and increased productivity, demonstrating how self-compassion can positively influence a collective environment.

Throughout this chapter, we have delved into the profound impact of self-compassion on mental health, the cultivation of resilient relationships, and the promotion of personal and professional growth. By adopting self-compassion, we not only enhance our own lives but also positively affect those around us.

As we draw this discussion to a close, we recognize that the path to emotional resilience and strength is deeply personal yet universally relevant. Looking ahead, the next chapter will explore how we can extend the principles of kindness and compassion beyond ourselves to cultivate supportive and empowering relationships. This next step ensures that the circle of compassion we've nurtured within ourselves expands to include our broader community, creating a network of allies who reflect our values and aspirations.

Chapter 8:

Crafting Your Circle: Knitting Together a Network of Authentic Allies

Navigating professional landscapes can sometimes leave us feeling isolated in our doubts and fears. By integrating into networks of support, we uncover the strength to combat these challenges head-on. These networks provide a foundation not just for personal validation but for shared growth, offering a mirror that reflects our true capabilities, often obscured by our doubts. Here, we discover how mentorship and open dialogues within these communities can act as catalysts for profound personal and professional transformation.

As we delve into the strategies and stories within this chapter, we are reminded that no one has to face their professional journey alone. The focus here is not merely on building networks but on nurturing meaningful connections that sustain us, inspire change, and empower us to redefine the boundaries of our potential. Join us as we explore how to effectively weave these connections into the fabric of our daily lives, turning every interaction into a stepping stone toward overcoming impostor syndrome and achieving collective success.

Cultivating Connections: Overcoming Doubts Together

Navigating the landscape of professional and personal challenges often leaves many of us feeling like impostors—outsiders in our own lives. This impostor syndrome finds fertile ground in isolation. However, by weaving strong networks of support and opening channels of communication, we can dismantle these doubts and foster a sense of belonging and confidence.

Community connections serve as a critical antidote to the isolation that amplifies impostor feelings. Being part of a supportive network where open discussions about insecurities are encouraged not only validates personal experiences but also diminishes the power of self-doubt. Establishing mentorship opportunities is particularly transformative. Mentors act as mirrors reflecting our true abilities and potential, often obscured by our doubts. They provide guidance, share insights, and reassure us against our baseless fears, helping to anchor our professional identity and growth.

Networking, whether through professional associations, social events, or online platforms, extends this concept. It allows for an exchange of experiences and strategies that demystify impostor syndrome and reinforce a collective resilience. These connections remind us that we are not alone in our experiences, providing both comfort and practical strategies for navigating our professional landscapes.

From understanding the power of mentorship and networking, we are reminded of the broader spectrum of support systems necessary for real change. Building diverse and inclusive networks is not just a strategy but a necessity for those seeking to thrive in varied professional landscapes. As we move into discussing these empowering networks, we continue to explore the rich benefits of diversity and the practical steps to achieving an inclusive support system.

Empowering Networks: The Power of Diverse and Inclusive Support

In the vast expanse of professional growth and personal development, establishing a diverse and inclusive support network is not just beneficial—it's essential. Because these networks are rich with varied perspectives and experiences, they enrich our understanding and amplify our resilience against the inevitable challenges we face—including those stemming from feelings of inadequacy or impostor syndrome. In this chapter, we explore how to construct and utilize such networks effectively, ensuring they serve not only as a safety net but also as a springboard for growth and empowerment.

Cultivating an Inclusive Network

Building a support system that transcends societal norms and expectations requires us to be intentional about inclusivity. It's important to push beyond the conventional boundaries set by societal roles or professional hierarchies and forge connections that reflect the true diversity of our communities and workplaces. These networks should not only support us in times of challenge but also challenge us to grow and think differently, offering new perspectives and insights that are crucial for personal and professional development.

For instance, mentorship programs tailored to embrace diversity can offer profound benefits. They connect individuals from various backgrounds, providing a richer mentorship experience characterized by a broad spectrum of advice and support. This approach not only helps mentees navigate their careers with more resilience but also enriches mentors' understanding and appreciation of different perspectives.

Transforming Challenges Into Opportunities

To illustrate the transformative power of a supportive network, consider the story of Wayne Sutton (2017), as detailed in his reflections on battling depression and impostor syndrome in the high-stakes environment of Silicon Valley. Wayne's journey underscores the critical role of self-awareness and community support in navigating the challenges that often accompany ambitious career paths. Despite his considerable achievements, Wayne faced profound emotional struggles that were exacerbated by the intense pressures of his industry.

His story is a stark reminder of the importance of having a support network that extends beyond professional guidance to emotional and mental health support. Wayne's experiences highlight how essential it is to cultivate networks that can provide not just career advice but also empathetic support and understanding of the personal challenges we face.

Building such a network involves several strategic steps:

1. **Proactive engagement:** Actively seek out and participate in networks that align with your values and goals. These networks might include professional associations, alumni groups, or online communities that focus on diversity and inclusion.

2. **Reciprocal relationships:** Foster relationships where both parties can offer and receive guidance. This reciprocal approach not only enhances the mentorship experience but also ensures that all members feel valued and supported.

3. **Comprehensive support systems:** Integrate emotional and mental health resources into your networks. This could involve setting up regular check-ins, sharing resources related to stress management, and creating spaces for open discussions about mental health.

Real-life narratives, such as Wayne's, serve not only as a testament to the challenges faced but also as a beacon of hope and a guide on how to navigate similar paths. His candid sharing of struggles provides a roadmap for integrating personal well-being with professional success and illustrates the profound impact of a supportive network. By openly discussing his journey, Wayne also contributes to a broader cultural shift toward acknowledging and addressing the often-taboo topics of mental health and impostor feelings in professional settings.

With these insights on building inclusive and diverse networks, we see how essential they are for personal resilience and professional advancement. But understanding these networks' transformative power only marks the beginning of their potential impact. Next, we will look into how these networks function within team dynamics and the strategies that can make these interactions more supportive and effective, fostering an environment that combats impostor syndrome from the ground up.

Fostering Team Resilience and Connection: A Comprehensive Approach

In the dynamic landscape of modern workplaces, fostering a culture that actively combats imposter syndrome through collaborative support and robust teamwork is not just beneficial—it's essential. This comprehensive approach not only enhances individual team members' sense of belonging and self-worth but also strengthens the entire organization's productivity and creativity.

Creating a Supportive Professional Environment

A supportive environment is foundational for mitigating the pervasive effects of imposter syndrome that many professionals face. To cultivate such an environment, it's crucial to implement several key practices:

- **Promoting open communication:** Encouraging an atmosphere where team members feel safe to express their thoughts and vulnerabilities is vital. This openness should be fostered by leaders modeling transparency and support, making it clear that the team values authenticity over perfection.

- **Implementing regular feedback sessions:** Constructive and regular feedback sessions are instrumental in providing team members with clear, actionable insights into their contributions. These sessions should focus on strengths as much as areas for improvement, helping individuals understand their value to the team and reducing feelings of inadequacy.

- **Celebrating achievements:** Making it a norm to recognize and celebrate each member's achievements can significantly boost morale and counteract imposter syndrome. This recognition should be both public and private, ensuring that all team members feel seen and appreciated.

- **Training for empathy:** Leadership training should emphasize empathy, teaching managers to recognize signs of imposter syndrome and respond appropriately. Empathetic leadership can make team members feel valued and understood, which is crucial for their personal growth and engagement.

Strategies for Effective Mentor-Mentee Relationships

Mentorship is a powerful tool in the professional world, providing guidance, knowledge, and emotional support. Effective mentor-mentee relationships are particularly critical for individuals struggling with feelings of impostor syndrome. Here's how to make the most of these relationships:

- **Establishing trust:** Trust is the cornerstone of any effective mentor-mentee relationship. Mentors should create a safe space where mentees can share their fears and challenges without judgment.

- **Setting realistic goals:** Together, mentors and mentees should set achievable, clear goals. This strategy helps mentees measure their progress and appreciate their successes, which is often difficult for those experiencing imposter syndrome.

- **Offering reassurance and perspective:** Mentors need to provide constant reassurance and a broader perspective on the mentee's experiences and feelings. Understanding that imposter syndrome is a common experience can normalize the feelings and reduce their intensity.

Navigating Team Dynamics and Power Imbalances

Imposter syndrome can both contribute to and be exacerbated by unequal power dynamics within a team. Addressing these imbalances involves these aspects:

- **Equitable opportunity:** Ensure that all team members, regardless of their level or background, have equal opportunities to contribute ideas and lead projects. This inclusivity can diminish feelings of being an "imposter" and empower all individuals to participate fully.

- **Encouraging vulnerability:** Creating a team culture where vulnerability is viewed as a strength can significantly improve team cohesion and support. It allows individuals to share their insecurities openly, thereby diminishing the power those insecurities have over them.

- **Fostering peer support:** Encourage the formation of peer support networks within the team. These groups can provide a space for sharing coping strategies and strengthening interpersonal relationships, enhancing the overall resilience of the team.

The strategies discussed here lay the groundwork for a team environment that not only acknowledges the challenges of impostor syndrome but actively combats them. As we conclude this section, we prepare to delve deeper into the practical tools and specific policies that can solidify this supportive culture. Our next focus will be on creating a comprehensive and nurturing workplace where everyone feels valued—a crucial step for personal and collective growth.

Cultivating Community and Fostering Belonging in the Workplace

In any professional setting, creating a culture that actively addresses impostor syndrome and fosters a strong sense of community and belonging is paramount. This not only enhances individual well-being but also bolsters collective success. Here, we delve into a cohesive strategy for building an inclusive and supportive workplace, blending various tools and approaches into a unified framework.

Strategic Implementation of Inclusive Practices

The foundation of a supportive work culture lies in its policies and practices. Establishing inclusive policies that embrace diversity in all its forms—gender, race, ethnicity, and more—ensures that every employee feels valued and empowered. Such policies should clearly articulate the organization's commitment to diversity and provide practical steps for addressing any instances of discrimination or bias.

Structured Mentorship Programs

Mentorship is a powerful tool for building confidence and a sense of belonging. By pairing newer employees with experienced mentors, organizations can provide newcomers with valuable insights and guidance, easing their transition into the corporate culture and reducing feelings of impostor syndrome. These relationships help mentees navigate the complexities of their new roles while gaining confidence in their abilities.

Team-Building for Stronger Connections

Beyond formal work tasks, fostering interpersonal relationships through regular team-building activities is crucial. These should be designed to be inclusive and engaging for everyone, potentially including group outings, team challenges, or social events. Such activities encourage casual interactions and deepen bonds, making the workplace a community where employees enjoy support and camaraderie.

Encouraging Collaborative Work Environments

Implementing group problem-solving sessions can significantly enhance teamwork and highlight the value of each team member's contributions. Such collaborations demonstrate the collective strength of the team and help individuals see how their ideas contribute to larger goals. Additionally, establishing peer review groups fosters a culture of continuous improvement and support, where feedback is seen as a tool for growth rather than criticism.

Understanding and Addressing the Impacts of Impostor Syndrome

Recognizing how impostor syndrome can affect teamwork and productivity is critical. It can lead individuals to undervalue their contributions or shy away from leadership opportunities, limiting both personal growth and team potential. To combat this, organizations can offer workshops focused on understanding and overcoming impostor syndrome, helping employees recognize their value and develop strategies to assert their capabilities.

Integration Through Educational Workshops

By conducting educational workshops that focus on the dynamics of impostor syndrome and the importance of a supportive work environment, we can achieve two important outcomes. Firstly, these sessions educate employees about impostor syndrome and how to overcome its challenges. Secondly, they empower employees to support one another in overcoming these challenges, thereby enhancing the overall health of the organization.

By blending these approaches into a cohesive strategy, we set the stage for a supportive work culture that extends beyond mere productivity. As we conclude this chapter on community and belonging, we pave the way for the next exciting chapter in our journey. In Chapter 9, we will apply these principles of support and collaboration to setting and achieving personal and professional goals, creating a clear and actionable blueprint for success that aligns with our values and aspirations. This transition not only builds on what we've learned but also focuses on practical application, ensuring that our newfound knowledge leads to tangible achievements.

Chapter 9:

Blueprinting Success: Navigating the Path to Your Ambitions

In this chapter, we delve into the critical process of setting and achieving meaningful goals—a cornerstone of personal and professional success. As you journey through these pages, you will learn to convert your aspirations into actionable steps, addressing and overcoming the psychological hurdles that often cloud our path, such as the ever-persistent shadows of self-doubt. This isn't just about reaching for the stars—it's about plotting a course that aligns deeply with who you are and what you truly want from life.

Setting goals is an art that requires clarity, precision, and a deep understanding of one's desires and capabilities. Here, we will explore how to identify what success truly means to you and how to systematically achieve it through well-defined, manageable steps. From understanding the nuances of effective goal-setting to celebrating each milestone along the way, this chapter is a guide to forging a path that is not only successful but also fulfilling and aligned with your deepest values.

Establishing a Foundation for Success

Achievement does not occur in a vacuum; it stems from a well-laid foundation that begins with a deep understanding of one's goals and aspirations. This chapter delves into the essential first step of any successful endeavor: setting meaningful goals. Here, we will explore how to define success tailored to your personal vision across different facets of your life, be it your career, personal development, or community involvement.

Defining Success: A Personalized Approach

Success is a subjective concept that varies dramatically from person to person. Understanding what success truly means to you is pivotal in crafting goals that resonate with your values and aspirations. Begin by reflecting on what you find fulfilling and rewarding. Ask yourself these questions:

- What achievements would make me truly proud?
- How do I want to impact my community or industry?
- What legacy do I wish to leave behind?

This reflection is not merely an exercise in thought but a crucial process in aligning your goals with your deepest values and desires. Whether it's reaching a professional milestone, achieving personal growth, or contributing to social change, the clarity gained from this exercise forms the cornerstone of your goal-setting strategy.

Utilizing SMART Criteria for Effective Goal Setting

To translate your vision of success into tangible outcomes, employ the SMART criteria:

- **Specific:** Clearly define what you want to accomplish, avoiding vague descriptions.

- **Measurable:** Set criteria for measuring progress and success.

- **Achievable:** Ensure that the goal is attainable with the resources and time you have.

- **Relevant:** Align each goal with your broader life objectives.

- **Time-bound:** Specify when the results can be achieved.

These criteria transform nebulous aspirations into clear, actionable goals. Complement this structured approach with a vision board—a dynamic and creative tool that visually represents your aspirations. By placing your vision board in a prominent location, you keep your goals constantly in sight, serving as a continuous source of motivation and focus.

Simplifying Complex Aspirations

Large goals can often be daunting, leading to procrastination or feelings of overwhelm. To manage your larger objectives, break them down into smaller, manageable tasks. This method allows each step to be clear and actionable, significantly reducing anxiety and making the journey toward large goals feel more attainable.

For instance, if your goal is to write a book, start by outlining chapters, then focus on writing one chapter at a time or even a few pages each day. This breakdown simplifies the process and keeps you moving forward step by step.

Developing Detailed Action Plans

With each small task identified, create a detailed action plan that includes the resources required, specific steps to be taken, and a timeline for completion. This plan acts as a roadmap, guiding you from start to finish and ensuring that each task is executed efficiently.

Monitoring Progress and Maintaining Engagement

Tracking your progress is critical in maintaining motivation and adapting your strategies as needed. Set regular intervals—whether weekly, monthly, or quarterly—to review your progress. These sessions provide an opportunity to celebrate accomplishments, reflect on challenges, and adjust your plans to better align with your goals.

Celebrating your successes, big or small, reinforces your confidence and commitment to your journey. It acknowledges your hard work and bolsters your morale, which is essential for long-term achievement.

Embracing a Holistic Approach to Achieving Goals

Achieving your goals isn't just about checking tasks off a list; it involves understanding and managing your emotional and psychological state throughout the journey. This includes recognizing potential challenges that may cloud your focus and employing strategies to navigate these challenges with resilience and clarity.

Engage in reflective practices such as journaling to document your thoughts, feelings, and insights. This not only helps in processing your experiences but also provides a motivational archive that can serve as a reminder of how far you've come and the lessons learned along the way.

Cultivating a Supportive Environment for Growth

No journey is solely individual. Building and using a supportive network of peers, mentors, and collaborators is crucial. This network not only provides encouragement but also offers diverse perspectives and collective wisdom essential for overcoming obstacles. Actively seek mentorship and engage in communities that resonate with your professional and personal ethos.

These relationships enrich your journey, offering support and accountability, which are vital for consistent progress. In this section, my aim is to equip you with the necessary tools and insights to transform your aspirations into tangible successes. By understanding the intricacies of goal-setting and the significance of a supportive framework, you can approach your ambitions with a renewed sense of purpose and clarity.

Navigating the Path to Your Ambitions: Overcoming Procrastination and Self-Doubt

In our pursuit of personal and professional goals, two formidable foes often emerge: procrastination and self-doubt. Both stem from deeper psychological patterns, including the fear of failure and imposter syndrome, which can profoundly affect our ability to set and achieve meaningful goals.

Procrastination is often misunderstood as mere laziness or poor time management. However, at its core, it is a complex psychological behavior typically driven by an underlying fear of failure or judgment. Recognizing procrastination as a manifestation of deeper fears is the first step in addressing it effectively. It's not about the inability to do the work; it's about the anxiety associated with the outcome of that work.

Visualization: A Tool for Clarity and Manifestation

Visualization is a potent technique to combat procrastination and manifest success. It involves vividly imagining not only achieving your goals but also the emotions that accompany these achievements. This method does more than inspire—it actively engages your brain in "encoding," a process where it maps out pathways to success as if you were experiencing it in reality.

Incorporate daily visualization practices where you see yourself overcoming obstacles and achieving your goals, feeling the joy and satisfaction that comes with each success. This dual focus on outcome and emotion ensures you are mentally and emotionally equipped for challenges, fostering a problem-solving mindset.

Consider Anita, a technology consultant whose journey was transformed by visualization. Each morning, she visualized her client meetings succeeding and projects completing flawlessly, immersing herself in feelings of confidence and accomplishment. This practice didn't just boost her self-esteem; it markedly enhanced her performance and client relations.

By integrating emotion into your visualization, you raise your vibrational frequency, aligning yourself more closely with your desires and dramatically increasing the likelihood of realizing your goals.

Tackling Imposter Syndrome and the Fear of Failure

Imposter syndrome is a common companion to procrastination. This syndrome can make goal-setting and decision-making daunting, as the fear of being "found out" can prevent taking any steps at all. Overcoming this starts with recognizing the achievements and capabilities you genuinely possess and understanding that perfection is neither possible nor necessary.

Creating a Roadmap: Guiding Your Journey

A well-defined roadmap is essential for navigating the journey to your goals. It acts not just as a planner but as a compass, providing clear direction and structured steps needed to reach your ultimate objectives. Each milestone on this roadmap should be actionable, accompanied by specific timelines and measurable metrics for success. This methodical approach ensures that every step taken is deliberate and brings you closer to your aspirations.

Detailing Your Roadmap

To effectively create your roadmap, start by defining your long-term goals and then break these down into smaller, more manageable objectives. For instance, if your goal is to advance to a leadership position within your company, your first step might involve undertaking leadership training or seeking mentorship opportunities within your organization. Follow this by outlining specific actions, such as leading a project team or enhancing your professional network. Assign realistic deadlines to each of these steps to keep yourself accountable and maintain momentum.

This roadmap should be regularly reviewed and updated to reflect your progress and any changes in your goals or circumstances. It serves not only as a reminder of where you're headed but also as a record of how far you've come, helping you stay focused and motivated.

Fostering Resilience and Determination

The path to achieving significant goals is rarely linear; it requires resilience and determination to navigate its highs and lows. Cultivating these qualities involves more than just enduring; it involves thriving amidst challenges. Mindfulness, for instance, is a powerful technique that helps anchor you in the present moment. It enhances your capacity to deal with stress and setbacks calmly and effectively. Practices such as daily meditation or mindful breathing exercises can integrate mindfulness into your routine, strengthening your emotional and psychological resilience.

Equally important is embracing a growth mindset—a belief that abilities and intelligence can be developed with effort, learning, and persistence. Viewing challenges as opportunities for growth rather than insurmountable obstacles can profoundly transform your approach to goal achievement. This mindset encourages experimentation, learning from failures, and viewing feedback as a precious resource for improvement rather than criticism.

Embracing Adaptability in Goal Pursuit

Adaptability is a critical skill in the modern world, where change is constant. Recognizing the need to pivot and adjust your strategies in response to changing circumstances is vital. This means regularly reassessing your goals and the effectiveness of your strategies. Being flexible allows you to respond to changes without significant disruptions to your progress, reducing the pressures that can feed procrastination and self-doubt.

Strategic Flexibility

To cultivate adaptability, develop a flexible plan that allows for adjustments. This plan might include setting aside time each month to review your goals and progress, being open to new opportunities that may arise unexpectedly, and being willing to abandon methods that are no longer effective. This flexible approach to goal setting and achievement ensures that you are not rigidly tied to one path but are prepared to take alternative routes to your destination.

Overcoming procrastination and self-doubt involves much more than willpower; it requires a deep understanding of your fears, strategic use of tools like visualization and planning, and a commitment to developing resilience and adaptability. By integrating these strategies, you set a solid foundation for success. As you advance on your journey, these principles will guide you, ensuring that every step is purposeful and aligned with your evolving ambitions. Keep these strategies at the forefront of your efforts, ready to adapt and overcome the challenges that may come your way. This proactive and dynamic approach ensures that your path to success is not only achievable but also rewarding.

Chapter 10:

Reframing Failure: A Journey through Resilience and Reinvention

Imagine standing at the crossroads of success and setback, where each failure holds the secret map to future triumphs. This realm, where challenges are embraced as mentors, invites you to transform your understanding and approach to professional hurdles. Through embracing our missteps and misfortunes, we gain invaluable insights that not only propel our careers forward but also enrich our personal growth.

This exploration into the heart of resilience reveals how setbacks, often cloaked in disappointment, are indeed hidden opportunities waiting to be uncovered and harnessed. Let's navigate these waters together, learning to turn the tides of failure into currents that guide us toward our true potential.

Reframing Failure as a Stepping Stone to Success

In navigating the twists and turns of professional and personal development, how we perceive and handle failure can profoundly influence our trajectory. Shifting our perspective to view failure not as a setback but as an indispensable part of growth can dramatically alter our approach to challenges, paving the way for innovation and success.

At the heart of every success story is a series of overlooked missteps and lessons learned. Failure is not just inevitable; it is essential to achieving profound success. By recognizing failure as a critical component of growth, we begin to dismantle the fears associated with setbacks, allowing us to approach our ambitions with resilience and creativity.

To genuinely embrace failure, we must foster a culture—both in our personal lives and within professional environments—that prioritizes learning and continuous improvement over mere perfection. This shift in mindset encourages innovation, reduces the stigma of failing, and promotes a more forgiving and ambitious pursuit of goals.

Learning from Setbacks: A Tactical Approach

Transforming failures into stepping stones requires a strategic and structured approach. Here's how you can effectively learn from setbacks:

1. **Conduct an analytical review:** After each failure, take a deep dive into what went wrong and why. This should be a non-judgmental process aimed at uncovering

actionable insights. Ask yourself these questions: What were the contributing factors? What can be retained that worked well?

2. **Develop actionable insights:** Use the insights from your analysis to adjust your methods or strategies. This process might mean tweaking your approach, adopting new techniques, or starting afresh with a more informed and refined plan.

Megan Dalla-Camina (2023b), a strategist, coach, and writer, has openly shared her journey through the treacherous waters of impostor syndrome. Megan's experience sheds light on the crucial role of self-acceptance and the perseverance needed to overcome deep-seated doubts and professional setbacks.

After years of struggling silently with feelings of inadequacy despite outward success, Megan reached a turning point where the only way forward was through radical self-acceptance and embracing her accomplishments. Her story is not just about personal triumph but also about the broader implications of fostering an environment where such challenges can be openly discussed and addressed.

Strategically Embracing Failure as a Catalyst for Growth

To cultivate a mindset that views failure as a growth opportunity, consider these strategies:

- **Develop a growth mindset:** Foster an attitude that thrives on challenges and views failure as a part of the learning curve. This mindset encourages continuous effort and adaptation, which are crucial for long-term achievement.

- **Effective risk assessment and mitigation:** Enhance your ability to evaluate risks and develop strategies to mitigate them. This proactive approach not only prepares you to handle potential setbacks better but also reduces the anxiety associated with taking on new challenges.

- **Implementing reframing techniques:** Regularly engage in reframing exercises that help shift your view of past failures from negative experiences to valuable lessons. This cognitive restructuring can profoundly affect how you approach future challenges.

- **Build supportive systems:** Cultivate a network that offers both encouragement and constructive feedback. Whether through mentors, peers, or professional groups, these relationships are vital for resilience, offering perspectives that can challenge your self-doubt and reinforce your capabilities.

By integrating these strategies, you can transform your response to failures, turning them into catalysts for innovation and growth. Embracing failure not only equips you with the resilience to navigate challenges but also empowers you to pursue your goals with a renewed sense of purpose and determination. This approach ensures that you are not merely surviving setbacks but thriving through them, setting a solid foundation for continued success in all areas of your life.

Risk-Taking Amidst Imposter Syndrome

Consider the experience of a manager facing a significant project setback. Rather than internalizing the failure as a reflection of her competence—a common reaction due to imposter syndrome—she takes a proactive approach. By analyzing the failure, identifying lessons learned, and sharing these insights with her team, she not only overcomes feelings of inadequacy but also reinforces her skills and leadership qualities.

Imposter syndrome can significantly influence our decision-making processes, often leading to either excessive caution or reckless behavior. Managing this imbalance is crucial for steady professional growth and personal satisfaction. By establishing a framework for calculated risk-taking and fostering an environment that provides supportive feedback, you can better navigate the complexities of decision-making while dealing with imposter syndrome.

Creating a nurturing environment where feedback is consistently constructive and supportive plays a crucial role in diminishing the impact of doubts during setbacks. Additionally, facilitating discussions within peer support groups, where members share their experiences with failure and imposter syndrome, can normalize these feelings and promote effective coping strategies.

Workshops focused on developing a growth mindset can be particularly effective. These workshops should include practical exercises that help participants reframe their view of setbacks, seeing them not as failures but as opportunities for growth and learning.

Understanding the Connection Between Imposter Syndrome and Risk-Taking

Understanding the link between imposter syndrome and risk-taking behaviors is crucial. Imposter syndrome may lead us to avoid taking any risks, fearing failure, or, conversely, to take reckless chances to overcompensate for feelings of fraudulence.

Finding a balance is essential for engaging in more measured and thoughtful risk-taking, which is crucial for growth.

Recognizing how imposter syndrome can lead to self-sabotaging behaviors is crucial for personal development. Initiatives that teach to recognize signs of self-sabotage and provide strategies to counter these behaviors can prevent them from undermining their own success.

In the journey through professional and personal challenges, stories of others who have successfully navigated similar paths can be incredibly powerful. For example, N.J. Lugo (2024) highlights individuals who embraced their imposter syndrome as part of their professional development. These narratives not only provide relatable and practical examples of overcoming adversity but also illustrate the transformative power of altering one's perspective toward failure.

Embracing Failure: A Catalyst for Growth and Innovation

Seeing failure as a crucial part of your journey toward success is transformative. It's not just about bouncing back; it's about extracting valuable lessons from each setback. When you dive deep into what went wrong—and what went right—you learn how to turn these insights into stepping stones for future successes. This process of reflection and learning builds a resilient mindset, enabling you to approach challenges not just as obstacles but as opportunities for innovation and self-improvement.

This perspective is vital not only for personal growth but also for exceeding your professional goals. Each failure, viewed as a lesson, enriches your journey, adding depth and resilience to your character. As we explore further, I'll show you how embracing this mindset prepares you to integrate self-compassion into your professional life, enhancing your ability to handle setbacks with grace and confidence.

Fostering Self-Compassion in Professional Contexts

Navigating professional landscapes often amplifies personal doubts, making setbacks feel challenging and overwhelmingly personal. Imposter syndrome can make these professional hurdles feel like profound emotional obstacles. As we work together in this chapter, I'll help you cultivate self-compassion, which is key to softening the internal criticism often accompanying these failures, and allow for a kinder, more objective perspective on these experiences.

You can significantly reduce self-judgment by integrating self-compassion exercises into your daily routine. One effective approach is mentally reframing failures. Instead of seeing a failed project or missed opportunity as a reaffirmation of imposter feelings, try viewing these instances as valuable learning experiences. This shift encourages a more forgiving internal dialogue and is crucial for navigating the emotional terrain of professional life. By establishing a routine of self-compassion, you arm yourself with the tools to handle the emotional repercussions of setbacks more effectively, not only soothing the sting of setbacks but also empowering you to move forward with resilience and a constructive perspective.

Leadership's Role in Cultivating a Learning Culture

As a leader—whether of a team or leading your own personal growth—you have the unique capacity to shape the culture around you to support risk-taking and value learning from setbacks. This reduces the fear of judgment and imposter syndrome, fostering an environment where everyone, including yourself, can thrive.

- **Encourage open conversations about failures:** Promoting a culture where failures and vulnerabilities can be discussed openly helps normalize these experiences and diminishes the stigma attached to them. This environment allows everyone, including you, to share and learn from each other's experiences, strengthening collective resilience.

- **Mentorship as a reflection tool:** Structured mentorship is transformative. If you are in a position to mentor, you provide not just guidance but also reassurance, helping to reshape the mentee's perception of their professional journey. If you're receiving mentorship, these relationships serve as mirrors, reflecting your true abilities that are often obscured by doubts.

To effectively manage and learn from failures, employing specific tools and strategies is essential:

- **Visualization techniques:** Visualizing both successful outcomes and potential setbacks prepares you mentally for actual scenarios. This practice helps in normalizing setbacks as part of the journey toward success, reducing their emotional impact.

- **After-action reviews (AAR):** For leaders, implementing regular AARs in your teams can turn setbacks into learning opportunities. These reviews focus on constructive feedback and are essential for developing future strategies that improve team performance. They provide a framework for you and your team to learn from each experience, reinforcing a culture that values growth and understanding.

In weaving these strategies into your professional life, whether as a leader of others or leading your own path, you foster an environment where self-compassion and understanding flourish. For deeper insights and more detailed strategies, consider exploring our companion journal. It offers further guidance on embedding these practices into your daily life, ensuring that the culture of learning and self-compassion you're developing continues to enrich both your personal and professional environments.

This approach not only helps you overcome personal and professional challenges but also establishes a solid foundation for lasting well-being and success, ensuring you can navigate life's stresses with grace and resilience.

A Pathway to Empowered Resilience

Embarking on this journey through our professional and personal landscapes, we've learned to harness the transformative power of setbacks, turning what once seemed like insurmountable obstacles into ladders reaching toward our goals. As we conclude this exploration, we emerge not just equipped with tools to tackle failure but with a renewed spirit, ready to approach each challenge as an opportunity for growth.

The lessons ingrained along this path do more than prepare us for future challenges; they reshape our perspective, nurturing a resilience that extends beyond professional boundaries into the essence of our personal lives.

As we transition into the next chapter of our journey, we focus on marrying our ambitions with our well-being, crafting a life where success is measured not just by achievements but by the joy and health with which we pursue them. This holistic approach ensures that our pursuits are sustainable and fulfilling, bringing harmony to our ambitious endeavors and the well-being that sustains them.

Chapter 11:

Fostering Harmony between Ambition and Well-Being

Ambition serves as the powerful engine behind our aspirations, propelling us toward achieving extraordinary heights. It ignites our passion, fuels our drive, and carves paths to remarkable successes. Yet, for many ambitious women, this forward thrust is often shadowed by a silent adversary: imposter syndrome. This psychological phenomenon, where individuals doubt their accomplishments and fear being exposed as a "fraud," disproportionately affects women, especially those striving to excel in their careers.

This chapter explores the intricate dance between high ambition and personal well-being. It's a journey through the internal conflict faced by many high-achieving women who wrestle with the fear that they don't truly deserve their success or that their achievements are the result of luck rather than skill. Such feelings can create a significant emotional and mental toll, undermining the very success they work so hard to achieve.

The presence of imposter syndrome can skew the perception of self-worth and amplify the stress associated with professional roles. As ambition pushes them to climb higher, the fear of being unmasked can lead to overwork, perfectionism, and an inability to reconcile their achievements with their self-image.

This not only stifles professional growth but also encroaches upon personal health and well-being.

The Delicate Balance: Ambition and Imposter Syndrome

Ambition and imposter syndrome frequently coexist in a paradoxical nexus that can be particularly intense for high-achieving individuals. The irony lies in the fact that the more one accomplishes, the greater the internal pressure and fear of being unmasked as a "fraud." This relentless drive can paradoxically lead to significant personal and professional setbacks if not managed carefully.

Ambition drives us to set and achieve high goals, but it often comes with an internal narrative that undermines these very achievements. The voice of imposter syndrome whispers doubts and fosters a fear that accomplishments are not genuinely deserved but are instead the result of serendipitous luck or timing. This section delves into the dynamic interplay between reaching for the stars and the fear of falling, illustrating how high achievers can reconcile their ambitions with their internal narratives.

Navigating Imposter Syndrome in Pursuit of Work-Life Balance

Imposter syndrome doesn't just complicate professional growth; it intricately affects personal lives, often urging individuals to sacrifice personal time in the guise of proving their worth. Recognizing this pattern is the first step toward cultivating a healthier approach to work-life balance.

Creating a culture of honest communication about career pressures and imposter feelings within professional settings can lead to more supportive work environments. Emphasizing the importance of life outside of work, encouraging time off, and recognizing personal milestones can help balance the scales.

Strategies for Achieving Sustainable Work-Life Balance

Achieving a sustainable balance between a demanding career and a fulfilling personal life is pivotal for mitigating the effects of imposter syndrome. Here are refined strategies to consider:

- **Setting clear work boundaries:** Define and communicate your work limits to colleagues and supervisors to protect your time and mental space.

- **Learning to say "no":** Empower yourself to decline additional responsibilities when your plate is full, focusing on quality over quantity in your professional undertakings.

- **Prioritizing time for rest and hobbies:** Ensure that leisure activities are part of your schedule, not an afterthought. Regularly engaging in hobbies and rest can recharge your mental batteries and improve overall productivity.

Cultivating Mental and Emotional Resilience

The cultivation of mental and emotional resilience is crucial in counteracting the stresses that accompany high levels of ambition:

- **Therapeutic interventions:** Regular sessions with a mental health professional can provide strategies to dismantle the imposter phenomenon and reinforce a positive self-image.

- **Social activities:** Maintaining an active social life can provide emotional support and decrease feelings of isolation often associated with imposter syndrome.

Implementing Practical Tools for Maintaining Healthy Boundaries

Implementing practical tools to maintain boundaries can significantly improve work-life balance:

- **Digital detoxes:** Regular intervals without electronic devices can help reduce stress and promote presence in personal interactions.

- **Clear work-hour limits:** Establish and adhere to specific work hours to prevent job demands from encroaching on personal time.

- **Scheduled "me-time":** Block off time in your calendar for activities that nourish your soul, treating these moments with the same importance as business meetings.

Natalie, a senior executive at a leading tech firm, candidly shares her journey toward balancing ambition with personal well-being. Overwhelmed by her rapid career advancement and plagued by doubts about her worthiness, Natalie faced burnout. Her turnaround began when she started scheduling monthly "well-being workshops" for herself—a time dedicated entirely to her personal growth and interests outside of work. This practice not only helped her manage her imposter feelings but also reaffirmed her non-work-related values and achievements. Natalie's story illustrates the transformative impact of taking deliberate steps to balance professional drive with personal care, showcasing a path that others might follow to harmonize their ambition with their well-being.

Through understanding and actively managing the relationship between ambition and imposter syndrome, we can foster a healthier professional environment and a more satisfying personal life, ultimately leading to a more balanced, fulfilling existence.

Imposter Syndrome in Career Aspirations: Bridging Self-Doubt With Success

The competitive landscape of your career often intensifies feelings of imposter syndrome. As you climb the professional ladder, each new level of achievement might paradoxically increase your self-doubt, clouding your recognition of personal accomplishments and casting a shadow over the very ambitions that fuel your progress. Such distorted perceptions can leave you feeling undeserving of your successes and uncertain of your skills.

The journey to overcoming imposter syndrome requires acknowledging these feelings as a common psychological phenomenon that does not reflect your true capabilities. Let's explore refined strategies that move beyond traditional approaches, helping you to reconcile high aspirations with a grounded sense of self-worth.

Strategic Self-Acknowledgment and Visualization

One innovative method to combat imposter feelings is strategic self-acknowledgment paired with visualization techniques. This method involves not just recognizing your achievements but also visually mapping them out in a timeline or achievement board. Seeing a visual representation of your success can reinforce the reality of your accomplishments, countering feelings of being an imposter. Regularly updating and reviewing this board serves as a constant, tangible reminder of your professional growth and worth.

Cultivating an Achievement-Oriented Mindset

To shift away from imposter syndrome, focus on cultivating an achievement-oriented mindset. This mindset involves setting specific, measurable goals and celebrating when you reach them, regardless of the scale. By focusing on what you have achieved—rather than how far you might still have to go—you reinforce your competence and capability in your professional role. This method helps recalibrate your self-perception to more accurately reflect your true professional stature.

Expanding Professional Development

Continuously expanding your professional development can also fortify your self-confidence. This process could involve pursuing certifications, attending workshops, or even cross-training in adjacent fields to broaden your understanding and skills. Each new skill acquired and every piece of knowledge gained contributes to a stronger, more confident professional identity, further dispelling imposter doubts.

Adaptive Resilience Practices

Building adaptive resilience practices is another essential strategy. This practice means developing the ability to adjust your workload and expectations based on your current mental and emotional capacity. It might involve setting boundaries or taking strategic breaks to prevent burnout. Learning to listen to your body and mind and responding with appropriate adjustments ensures that you maintain your professional performance without compromising your well-being.

Networking and Collaborative Achievements

Engaging more deeply with your professional network can also diminish feelings of fraudulence. Collaborative projects highlight the value of your contributions in a team setting, providing direct feedback and validation from peers. These interactions not only enhance your professional network but also embed a deeper sense of belonging and legitimacy in your industry.

Consider Lisa, a corporate executive whose rise to the top was nearly derailed by her struggles with imposter syndrome. Lisa adopted a method of strategic self-acknowledgment and expanded her professional development to encompass leadership in non-profit organizations, enhancing her sense of worth and competency. Her success story illustrates that with the right strategies, aligning your self-perception with reality and embracing your success with confidence is not only possible but within your reach.

By integrating these strategies, you lay the groundwork for long-term success and fulfillment in your career. For further exploration of these concepts, consider consulting the companion journal, which offers deeper insights and structured exercises to support your journey. Remember, overcoming imposter syndrome is not about silencing self-doubt entirely but transforming it into a motivational force that drives personal and professional growth.

Rising Above

In our exploration of the complex dance between ambition and imposter syndrome, we've uncovered how high achievers often face an internal battle between their aspirations and the doubts that accompany their successes. This paradox can undermine well-being and professional growth, making it crucial to address these feelings directly.

Rather than succumbing to self-doubt, adopting strategic self-affirmation and focusing on continuous professional development can shift perceptions and reinforce a healthy self-image. Visualizing achievements and setting clear, measurable goals help ground ambition in reality, affirming that successes are well-deserved.

These strategies are not just coping mechanisms but are transformative in aligning our professional trajectories with genuine self-perception. By embracing our achievements and continually seeking growth, we can navigate the challenges of imposter syndrome with confidence and grace.

As we move into the next chapter, we'll explore how to deepen these strategies, enhancing your resilience and self-assurance. This next step will focus on enduring practices that support ongoing personal and professional development, ensuring you're equipped to handle future challenges with confidence and clarity.

Chapter 12:

Cultivating Lasting Confidence and Dynamic Growth

If you've ever climbed a mountain, you know the summit isn't the end of the journey—it's a brief pause to enjoy the view before you head back down, equipped with the knowledge and confidence gained from the ascent. Similarly, as we reach the final chapter of our book, think of it not as a conclusion but as a vantage point. From here, we can see how far we've come and prepare for the trails still ahead.

This chapter extends beyond just reviewing the progress we've made in overcoming imposter syndrome. It aims to transform our newfound resilience and self-assurance into catalysts for sustained growth. We'll develop a durable framework that incorporates these strengths into every facet of our daily lives, both personal and professional.

Together, we'll develop a sustainable framework for growth that goes beyond overcoming temporary challenges. We will establish lifelong strategies that ensure you not only maintain the confidence you've built but also continue to expand it. Let's explore how to embed these strategies into your routine, ensuring that each step forward makes you stronger and more adept at navigating future paths, whatever they may be.

Creating a Long-Term Plan for Self-Confidence

Building lasting self-confidence transcends occasional triumphs over doubts; it's about crafting a lifelong strategy for personal empowerment that grows with you. This approach includes cultivating habits and practices that foster self-assurance, preparing you to tackle future challenges and seize opportunities for growth.

Dynamic Goal Setting

True confidence emerges from a pattern of setting and achieving goals that are tailored to your evolving skills and life circumstances. It's about understanding where you are now and envisioning where you want to be, then building the bridge between these points with carefully chosen milestones. This dynamic goal-setting process encourages a continuous growth mindset that evolves as you do, pushing you to expand your boundaries and explore new possibilities.

To embed this into your life, begin by assessing your current achievements and setting immediate short-term goals. As you accomplish these goals, celebrate your successes and then set your sights on more challenging objectives. This cycle of planning, achieving, and revising not only boosts your self-confidence but also ensures that your growth trajectory remains ambitious and achievable.

Cultivating Effective Feedback Loops

Feedback is the mirror that reflects your growth trajectory and helps adjust your path. Constructive feedback, whether from peers, mentors, or your self-reflection, is vital for personal and professional development. It acts as a reality check that helps you understand your strengths and areas for improvement, providing a balanced perspective on your achievements and the areas where you can grow.

To make the most of feedback, establish regular check-ins with mentors who can provide insights based on their experiences, offering guidance that resonates with your personal challenges and aspirations. Similarly, cultivate a habit of seeking feedback from colleagues and supervisors, ensuring that it's a two-way conversation where you can discuss achievements and set goals for future improvement. Additionally, engage in reflective practices like journaling or meditative contemplation to personally assess your progress and set self-directed goals.

Integrating Self-Reflection and Adaptation

Incorporate self-reflection into your routine to make self-assessment a natural part of your growth process. Regularly take time to reflect on your successes and the challenges you've faced. This could be through writing, meditation, or even discussions with a trusted friend or advisor. Use these reflections to adjust your goals and strategies, ensuring they remain aligned with your evolving self-understanding and life circumstances.

Adaptation is equally critical. As you progress in your personal and professional life, remain flexible to change directions or strategies as needed. Life's unpredictability means that the path to your goals may need recalibrating. Embrace this as an opportunity to develop resilience and learn new skills rather than a setback.

By establishing a long-term plan that emphasizes dynamic goal setting, effective feedback loops, and continuous self-reflection and adaptation, you create a robust framework for sustained self-confidence. This approach ensures that your journey toward personal empowerment is not just reactive to immediate challenges but is a proactive, evolving strategy that prepares you for whatever the future holds.

Ongoing Practices for Maintaining a Positive Self-Image

A positive self-image is foundational to sustained self-confidence. It shapes how you perceive and react to challenges, influences your interactions with others, and propels you toward your goals. Cultivating and maintaining a positive self-image requires consistent effort and the integration of practices that reinforce your sense of self-worth and capability.

Integrating Affirmation Routines Into Daily Life

Affirmations are powerful tools for reshaping thoughts and reinforcing a positive self-image. They work by systematically replacing the negative self-talk that often undermines confidence with positive, empowering statements that celebrate your strengths and achievements. To effectively integrate affirmations into your daily routine, consider setting aside specific times during the day for reflection—perhaps in the morning as you prepare for the day or in the evening as you wind down.

Use affirmations that are specific to your achievements and aspirations, such as, "I am skilled and my work creates value," or, "I am capable of overcoming any challenges that come my way." Over time, these affirmations can shift your internal dialogue from doubt to confidence, profoundly influencing how you view yourself and your capabilities.

Harnessing the Power of Visualization

Visualization goes hand-in-hand with affirmations but taps into the brain's capacity to simulate experiences, making success feel more attainable. By regularly envisioning yourself achieving your goals, overcoming obstacles, and handling challenging interactions with grace and competence, you begin to solidify these outcomes in your mind as not only possible but expected.

To practice visualization effectively, create a quiet space where you can concentrate without interruptions. Close your eyes and imagine a scene in which you are successfully executing a task or achieving a goal. Focus on the details—envision the setting, the actions you are taking, the responses of others, and most importantly, the emotions you are feeling. This practice enhances your mental and emotional resilience, preparing you to face real-world challenges with increased confidence.

Creating a Synergy Between Affirmations and Visualization

To maximize the impact of these techniques, combine them into a cohesive routine. Start with affirmations to set a positive tone, reinforcing your belief in your abilities and worth. Follow up with visualization, where you not only see yourself succeeding but also mentally rehearse the steps involved in that success. This combination not only boosts your confidence but also prepares you mentally and emotionally for the actions you need to take in reality.

Maintaining a positive self-image is more than just a self-help strategy; it's a profound transformation of your internal narrative. These practices equip you with the tools to confidently approach challenges, enhance your interactions, and actively move toward your goals. Over time, they become integrated into your daily life, continuously reinforcing a self-image that supports sustained confidence and growth.

Encouraging Continuous Personal and Professional Development

In a world where change is the only constant, dynamic growth is crucial for maintaining relevance and excellence in both our personal and professional lives. Embracing this change requires a proactive approach to development, one that continually evolves to meet new challenges and seize emerging opportunities. This ongoing process of growth isn't just about reacting to changes—it's about anticipating and shaping them to fit your vision and goals.

Embracing Lifelong Learning

Lifelong learning is the cornerstone of continuous development. It's about maintaining a curious and open mindset, ready to absorb new information and skills regardless of your age or career stage. This commitment to learning can take various forms, from formal academic courses leading to degrees and certifications to more flexible arrangements like online courses, workshops, seminars, and extensive reading.

The key is to tailor your learning experiences to align with your career goals and personal interests. For instance, if you're in a technology-driven field, staying updated with the latest technological advances through specialized courses or certifications can be crucial. Conversely, if you're looking to expand into leadership roles, you might focus on workshops that enhance your communication and strategic thinking skills.

Here are some strategies to integrate lifelong learning into your routine:

- **Scheduled learning sessions:** Dedicate specific times in your week for learning new skills or updating existing ones. Treat these sessions with the same importance as a business meeting.

- **Diverse learning sources:** Combine various learning sources to keep the process engaging. Utilize books, online courses, podcasts, webinars, and even thoughtful discussions with peers as learning tools.

- **Apply learning practically:** Ensure that the knowledge you gain is not just theoretical. Find ways to apply new skills in your current role or projects, which can also help in retaining what you learn.

Developing Adaptability

Adaptability is an essential skill in modern workplaces and our personal lives. It involves more than just reacting to changes—it requires proactive anticipation and strategic preparation for various scenarios.

To enhance your adaptability, engage in these activities:

- **Scenario planning:** Regularly set aside time to imagine potential future scenarios and develop plans to address them. This process could involve brainstorming sessions either solo or with a team to cover various "what if" situations.

- **Role-playing exercises:** These exercises can be particularly useful for developing interpersonal skills and preparing for different social or professional interactions. Role-playing can help you navigate complex conversations and improve your ability to think on your feet.

- **Strategic forecasting:** Use tools and methods to predict future trends in your industry or life. This process can help you prepare for changes and ensure that your skills and strategies are aligned with future needs.

Encouraging continuous personal and professional development is about creating a lifestyle that embraces learning and adaptability as core principles. By integrating these elements into your daily routines and strategic planning, you ensure that you are not only prepared for the future but are also actively shaping it to your advantage. This proactive approach to development fosters a resilient and versatile personal and professional life, capable of thriving in an ever-changing world.

Strategies for Sustaining Confidence and Growth Beyond Overcoming Imposter Syndrome

Moving beyond imposter syndrome requires embedding enduring strategies into your lifestyle that not only prevent its recurrence but also strengthen your psychological and emotional foundations to meet future challenges head-on. This approach entails a deeper, more ingrained method of cultivating resilience and fostering a cycle of continuous personal growth and mentoring.

Cultivating Resilience Through Workshops

Participating in resilience workshops is a proactive way to build your emotional and psychological strengths, which are key to maintaining confidence and supporting long-term development. These workshops are designed to provide comprehensive training that helps you understand stress triggers, manage adverse situations, and develop coping mechanisms that enhance your ability to bounce back from setbacks.

The focus of these workshops extends beyond simple skill-building; they aim to transform your approach to challenges, encouraging a mindset that views difficulties as growth opportunities rather than insurmountable obstacles. By regularly engaging in such training, you embed resilience into your daily habits and thought processes, which is crucial for sustaining personal growth and confidence.

Enhancing Growth Through Mentorship Roles

Taking on mentorship roles offers a unique opportunity to reinforce your own growth while contributing to the development of others. By teaching and guiding peers or less experienced professionals, you not only consolidate your own knowledge and skills but also enhance your self-confidence. Mentorship allows you to see the practical impact of your expertise and experience through others' successes, which in turn reaffirms your own capabilities and achievements.

Moreover, mentorship creates a feedback loop where the mentor often learns from the mentee, gaining new perspectives and ideas. This role reinforces your professional identity and strengthens your leadership qualities, making you more resilient to imposter syndrome and self-doubt.

Recognizing and Managing the Long-Term Impact of Imposter Syndrome

Imposter syndrome is a pervasive challenge that can skew your long-term self-perception, influencing everything from your daily choices to your overall career trajectory. To counteract its effects, it's crucial to weave self-awareness practices into your daily routine, recognizing and addressing feelings of self-doubt early before they can impact your confidence and decision-making.

Self-awareness can be deepened through innovative methods such as narrative therapy, which uses storytelling to help you understand and reshape your identity, and role-playing different decision-making scenarios to build confidence and assertiveness. These techniques encourage a reflective examination of your thoughts and emotions, allowing for a more accurate alignment of your self-perception with your true abilities.

Consider Rene, whose professional journey encapsulates the essence of resilience and adaptability. Initially constrained within the corporate world, Rene felt a deep desire to make a direct impact on her community, which led her to launch her own tech startup. This bold move was just the beginning of her transformative path. After her startup successfully launched its flagship product, she pivoted toward social entrepreneurship, leveraging her technology to address educational disparities.

Rene's story is a powerful testament to the importance of continual growth and adaptation. Her willingness to evolve her goals and embrace new challenges allowed her to navigate various professional landscapes successfully.

Incorporating these introspective practices consistently helps establish a dynamic framework that bolsters your self-worth and equips you to face future challenges with strength and clarity. This approach ensures that your journey toward personal and professional development is progressive and rewarding, significantly reducing the space for imposter syndrome to flourish.

Strategies for Sustained Growth and Adaptability

To effectively manage career fluctuations and the uncertainties of professional life, developing resilience and adaptability is essential. One effective approach is engaging in cross-functional training or participating in interdisciplinary projects, which can diversify your skills and reinforce your professional confidence.

Fostering a strong professional network and engaging in collaborative projects can affirm your role and reduce feelings of fraudulence. These interactions not only enhance your professional network but also deepen your sense of legitimacy and belonging in your industry.

By stepping into collaborative roles and seeking feedback, you affirm your contributions and solidify your professional identity, which can significantly diminish the impact of imposter syndrome.

Wrapping Up and Looking Ahead

As we wrap up this discussion, it's important to reflect on the strategies discussed as foundational, not just for overcoming temporary challenges but for enabling a lifetime of growth and success. These principles are designed to help you thrive amidst challenges, fostering a resilient and adaptable professional persona.

For those looking to delve deeper into these topics, the companion journal offers extensive resources and exercises designed to reinforce the strategies discussed here. This guide serves as a valuable tool for anyone seeking to continue their journey of personal and professional development, providing structured guidance to navigate the complexities of career growth and self-improvement.

This chapter is not merely a conclusion but a launchpad for your continued growth, urging you to keep growing and embracing each challenge as an opportunity to learn and expand. Embrace this journey with the confidence and curiosity that has brought you this far, and be ready to explore new horizons that lie ahead.

Conclusion

As we bring our journey together to a close, reflect on the transformative path we've navigated—from confronting the shadows of doubt to embracing the full spectrum of our potential. We have ventured beyond the surface of traditional success metrics to explore a deeper, more authentic form of achievement—one that aligns with our core values and true self.

Throughout this book, we've uncovered strategies to dismantle the barriers of imposter syndrome, redefined our understanding of failure and success, and learned to cultivate resilience in the face of adversity. More importantly, we've discovered how embracing our authentic selves can lead to profound fulfillment and effectiveness, both personally and professionally.

Now, as you move forward, I encourage you to take these lessons and apply them to your own life. Reflect on your actions, reassess your goals, and realign your paths whenever necessary. Use the insights and strategies explored here to continuously foster an environment of growth and self-acceptance. Challenge yourself to remain committed to your journey of self-discovery and to constantly seek ways to live more authentically.

Let this book be a starting point—not a conclusion. Carry forward the courage to question, the strength to challenge, and the confidence to be true to yourself. Step boldly into your potential, equipped with the tools to transform challenges into opportunities for growth. Remember, every day is a chance to rewrite the narrative of your life into one that resonates with the depth of your true aspirations.

Thank you for sharing this journey with me. May the lessons learned illuminate your path forward and inspire you to continuously craft a life that is not only successful by external standards but deeply fulfilling by your own definition. Keep moving forward, keep growing, and most importantly, keep being real.

References

Adegbile, M. (2023, May 12). *Embracing failure: Strategies for women to build confidence and resilience*. ESMT Berlin Blog. https://blog.esmt.berlin/voices/embracing-failure-strategies-for-women-to-build-confidence-and-resilience/

Alcock, D. (2022, April 4). *Self-limiting beliefs and imposter syndrome*. Linkedin. https://www.linkedin.com/pulse/self-limiting-beliefs-imposter-syndrome-david-alcock#:~:text=One%20of%20the%20biggest%20challenges

Ascent Global Partners. (2024, February 1). *Overcoming imposter syndrome: Strategies for building confidence and conquering self-doubt*. Linkedin. https://www.linkedin.com/pulse/overcoming-imposter-syndrome-strategies-building-sp1bc?trk=article-ssr-frontend-pulse_more-articles_related-content-card

Avrachan, A. (2023, October 31). *Overcoming imposter syndrome: Building confidence and embracing success in the workplace*. Great Place to Work. https://www.greatplacetowork.in/overcoming-imposter-syndrome-building-confidence-and-embracing-success-in-the-workplace

Beranek, C. (2023, June 14). *Imposter syndrome predominantly affects women — here's how to overcome it*. Entrepreneur. https://www.entrepreneur.com/leadership/imposter-syndrome-predominantly-affects-women-heres/453161#:~:text=Often%2C%20imposter%20syndrome%20is%20an

Best practice: Developing resilience and overcoming imposter syndrome. (n.d.). Arizona State University. https://graduate.asu.edu/graduate-insider/best-practice-developing-resilience-and-overcoming-imposter-syndrome

Blumberg, N. (2023). Malala Yousafzai. In *Encyclopedia Britannica.* https://www.britannica.com/biography/Malala-Yousafzai

Boisvert, J. (2022, March 1). *Imposter syndrome: The importance of developing A support system.* The PhD Place. https://thephdplace.com/imposter-syndrome-the-importance-of-developing-a-support-system/

Bonholzer, B. (2023, February 28). *Strategies to navigate imposter syndrome & self-limiting beliefs.* Linkedin. https://www.linkedin.com/pulse/strategies-navigate-imposter-syndrome-self-limiting-bjorn

Brichard, C. (2021, October 7). *Overcome your imposter syndrome and other limiting beliefs.* Medium. https://medium.com/@camillebrichard/overcome-your-imposter-syndrome-and-other-limiting-beliefs-69551fde598f

Brookman, S. (2022, December 5). *Why imposter syndrome affects female leaders more than men.* Medium. https://medium.com/real-life-resilience/why-imposter-syndrome-affects-female-leaders-more-than-men-962abcea8983

Brown, M. (2024, February 25). *Overcoming imposter syndrome: Strategies for embracing your achievements*. Juniper Counseling. https://junipercounseling.org/overcoming-imposter-syndrome-strategies-for-embracing-your-achievements/

Cai, C. (2022, August 11). *Processing my experience with imposter syndrome*. CodeX. https://medium.com/codex/processing-my-experience-with-imposter-syndrome-53c546c1be3

Campbell, C. (2021). *The struggle is real: The imposter syndrome and the university experience of black female students at chico state* [Thesis]. https://scholarworks.calstate.edu/downloads/7d279046d

Caprino, K. (2022, October 22). *Impostor syndrome prevalence in professional women and how to overcome it*. Forbes. https://www.forbes.com/sites/kathycaprino/2020/10/22/impostor-syndrome-prevalence-in-professional-women-face-and-how-to-overcome-it/?sh=6b841c73cbd9

Coping with imposter syndrome & appropriate goal-setting. (2024, April 15). Annabelle Psychology. https://www.annabellepsychology.com/coping-with-imposter-syndrome-appropriate-goalsetting

Coursera Staff. (2023, November 29). *What is imposter syndrome (and how to overcome it)?* Coursera. https://www.coursera.org/articles/imposter-syndrome

Cuncic, A. (2022, November 17). *What is imposter syndrome?* Verywell Mind. https://www.verywellmind.com/imposter-syndrome-and-social-anxiety-disorder-4156469

Cyrankiewicz, J. (2024, January 8). *Imposter syndrome — doing & iterating vs overthinking (and not doing at all)*. Medium. https://medium.com/@justynacyrankiewicz/imposter-syndrome-doing-iterating-vs-overthinking-and-not-doing-at-all-7a89e0cc48e

Dalla-Camina, M. (2023a, June 26). *Overcoming imposter syndrome: Embracing your achievements with confidence*. Women Rising. https://womenrisingco.com/articles/overcoming-imposter-syndrome-embracing-your-achievements-with-confidence/

Dalla-Camina, M. (2023b, June 28). *Overcoming imposter syndrome: Embracing your achievements with confidence*. Linkedin. https://www.linkedin.com/pulse/overcoming-imposter-syndrome-embracing-your-megan-dalla-camina

Dalla-Camina, M. (2023c, July 14). *Overcoming imposter syndrome*. Psychology Today Australia. https://www.psychologytoday.com/au/blog/real-women/202306/overcoming-imposter-syndrome

Delia, S. (2023, August 23). *Overcome imposter syndrome in personal & professional realms*. Delia Counseling Services. https://deliacounselingservices.com/embracing-your-worth-empowering-women-to-overcome-imposter-syndrome-in-personal-professional-realms/

Diamond, T. Y. (2023, November 23). *Embracing your potential: Overcoming imposter syndrome*. Medium. https://dreamchasersradio.medium.com/embracing-your-potential-overcoming-imposter-syndrome-f15dd9e821e3

Dominguez-Salazar, K., Van, R., & Pharmd, V.-D. (n.d.). *Imposter syndrome workshop: Impact and overcoming learning objectives*.

https://www.nmpharmacy.org/resources/Documents/Imposter%20Experience_NMPhA_2023-Final61523%206%20slides%20per%20pg.pdf

Downie, M. (2022, January 12). *Helping team members deal with imposter syndrome*. Mark Downie. https://www.poppastring.com/blog/helping-team-members-deal-with-imposter-syndrome

Effective ways to overcome imposter syndrome. (2023, August 21). Women on Topp. https://www.womenontopp.com/10-most-effective-ways-to-overcome-imposter-syndrome/

Eriksson, K., Persson, E., & Stenkil, E. (2023). *The Effects of Impostor Syndrome on Swedish Women in Leadership Positions NUMBER OF CREDITS: 15 credits PROGRAMME OF STUDY: International Management*. https://www.diva-portal.org/smash/get/diva2:1764575/FULLTEXT01.pdf

5 strategies for turning imposter syndrome into a stepping stone. (2023, October 12). Her New Standard. https://hernewstandard.com/overcoming-imposter-syndrome-strategies-for-women-leaders/

Ford, H. (n.d.). *A quote by Henry Ford*. GoodReads. https://www.goodreads.com/quotes/106813-the-only-real-mistake-is-the-one-from-which-we

former_member181891. (2018, September 13). *Identifying and overcoming impostor syndrome*. SAP Community. https://community.sap.com/t5/welcome-corner-blog-posts/identifying-and-overcoming-impostor-syndrome/ba-p/13374704

Gharaei, M. (2021, February 2). *How to recognise and overcome imposter syndrome*. The Female Factor. https://www.femalefactor.global/post/recognise-and-overcome-imposter-syndrome

Hammond, K. E. (2023, March 15). *Despite professional successes many women still experience imposter syndrome*. The Survey Center on American Life. https://www.americansurveycenter.org/women-are-achieving-greater-professional-success-yet-self-doubt-is-common/

Harlow, L. (2021, March 16). *Surviving imposter syndrome*. Age of Awareness. https://medium.com/age-of-awareness/how-imposter-syndrome-took-over-my-life-f873146863b4

Hirsh, R. (2024, January 8). *Navigating imposter syndrome on the path to success: A guide for students*. Mary Baldwin University. https://life-success.marybaldwin.edu/blog/2024/01/08/navigating-imposter-syndrome-on-the-path-to-success-a-guide-for-students/

Hodde Miller, S. (n.d.). *Imposter syndrome*. Propel Women. https://www.propelwomen.org/content/imposter-syndrome/gjeb3f

How can external support and mentorship help you overcome imposter syndrome? (2019). Quora. https://www.quora.com/How-can-external-support-and-mentorship-help-you-overcome-imposter-syndrome

How can I overcome impostor syndrome and gain confidence in my abilities as an entrepreneur? (2019). Quora. https://www.quora.com/How-can-I-overcome-impostor-syndrome-and-gain-confidence-in-my-abilities-as-an-entrepreneur

How to break free from imposter syndrome. (2023, July 9). Amy Rose Therapy. https://amyrosetherapy.co.uk/how-to-break-free-from-imposter-syndrome/

How to combat imposter syndrome. (2023, June 11). MotivatHER. https://motivather.com/how-to-combat-imposter-syndrome/

How to Crush Your Imposter Syndrome and Limiting Beliefs. (2020, August 4). FastForwardAmy . https://fastforwardamy.com/how-to-crush-your-imposter-syndrome-and-limiting-beliefs-fastforwardamy-show-episode-34/

How to overcome impostor syndrome in business? (2024, February 8). CIO Women Magazine. https://ciowomenmagazine.com/overcome-impostor-syndrome-in-business/

Huecker, M. R., Shreffler, J., McKeny, P. T., & Davis, D. (2023). *Imposter phenomenon.* PubMed; StatPearls Publishing. https://www.ncbi.nlm.nih.gov/books/NBK585058/#:~:text=Introduction

Imposter syndrome. (n.d.). FasterCapital. https://fastercapital.com/keyword/imposter-syndrome-imposter-syndrome.html

Imposter syndrome is sexist, actually: Embracing your feelings as protest. (2022, November 1). Bookish Brews. https://bookishbrews.com/overcoming-imposter-syndrome/

Imposter syndrome: A creative's struggle. (n.d.). Digital Panda Blogs. https://www.thedigitalpanda.com/blog/imposter-syndrome-a-creative-struggle

Imposter syndrome: What is it and how can it impact your career? (2023, March 17). N26.com. https://n26.com/en-eu/blog/imposter-syndrome

Izobel. (2024, March 8). *Up & about: How to overcome fear of failure & imposter syndrome (as a type A girlie).* Up & About. https://sites.libsyn.com/480168/how-to-overcome-fear-of-failure-imposter-syndrome-as-a-type-a-girlie

Jackson, S. (2023, August 7). *High-Performing women and the imposter syndrome.* Linkedin. https://www.linkedin.com/pulse/high-performing-women-imposter-syndrome-scharrell-jackson

John. (2021, July 11). *The truth about "imposter syndrome."* Girls in Tech. https://girlsintech.org/blog/the-truth-about-imposter-syndrome/

Leeman, J. (2023, November 2). *Dealing with imposter syndrome.* Linkedin. https://www.linkedin.com/pulse/dealing-imposter-syndrome-joel-leeman--sqx4c

Li, D. (2022, June 13). *Combating the imposter syndrome as a leader.* Medium. https://danjueli.medium.com/combating-the-imposter-syndrome-as-a-leader-397fa92f0df4

Liu, L., Han, Y., Lu, Z., Cao, C., & Wang, W. (2022). The relationship between perfectionism and depressive symptoms among Chinese college students: The mediating roles of self-compassion and impostor syndrome. *Current Psychology.* https://doi.org/10.1007/s12144-022-03036-8

Loh, G. (2024, March 3). *Shattering expectations & confronting imposter syndrome in professional women.* Counseling Perspective. https://www.counselingperspective.com/shattering-expectations-confronting-imposter-syndrome-in-professional-women

Lugo, N. J. (2024, March 6). *Embracing imposter syndrome.* Medium. https://medium.com/@bluepeakstrategy/embracing-imposter-syndrome-78e5cfa03473

Mai, T., & Zamora, E. (n.d.). *You're not alone in your imposter syndrome.* Accelerate. https://accelerate.uofuhealth.utah.edu/equity/you-re-not-alone-in-your-imposter-syndrome

Mendoza, C. (2014, November 20). *Overcoming imposter syndrome.* Mayo Clinic. https://educationdiversityblog.mayo.edu/2014/11/20/overcoming-imposter-syndrome/

Mental health awareness week: Battling imposter syndrome. (2023, May 16). Team ITG. https://teamitg.com/mental-health-awareness-week-battling-imposter-syndrome/

Miles, S. (n.d.). *Overcoming imposter syndrome: empowering female founders to embrace their skills and achievements.* Startups Magazine. https://startupsmagazine.co.uk/article-overcoming-imposter-syndrome-empowering-female-founders-embrace-their-skills-and

Mind Tools Content Team. (n.d.). *Impostor syndrome.* Mind Tools. https://www.mindtools.com/azio7m7/impostor-syndrome

Moody, L. (2022, June 8). *How to overcome imposter syndrome on the healthier together podcast.* Liz Moody. https://www.lizmoody.com/healthiertogetherpodcast-how-to-overcome-imposter-syndrome/

Mou, M. (2023, November 15). *How to overcome imposter syndrome and thrive in the tech world.* University of London. https://www.london.ac.uk/news-events/student-blog/how-overcome-imposter-syndrome-thrive-tech-world

Mwaura, M. (2022, May 18). *Embracing imposter syndrome: How to quiet your inner mean girl.* Linkedin. https://www.linkedin.com/pulse/embracing-imposter-syndrome-how-quiet-your-inner-mean-maryanne-mwaura

Nance-Nash, S. (2020, July 28). *Why imposter syndrome hits women and women of colour harder.* BBC. https://www.bbc.com/worklife/article/20200724-why-imposter-syndrome-hits-women-and-women-of-colour-harder

Nicols, B. (n.d.). *Imposter syndrome affects 65% of professionals, new study finds.* PR NewsWire. https://www.prnewswire.com/news-releases/imposter-syndrome-affects-65-of-professionals-new-study-finds-301295516.html

Northeastern Alumni. (2023, November 3). *Cultivating balance and combatting burnout and impostor syndrome.* Youtube. https://www.youtube.com/watch?v=iRP8uIcWKec

Nour, D. (2024, January 27). *When the imposter syndrome stunts your growth.* Forbes. https://www.forbes.com/sites/davidnour/2024/01/27/when-the-imposter-syndrome-stunts-your-growth/?sh=49a4a8c117ab

Olowookere, B. (2024, January 15). *Embracing imposter syndrome: A path to authentic success.* Medium. https://medium.com/@jideolowookere/embracing-imposter-syndrome-a-path-to-authentic-success-3525981d0a0b

Oniyitan, O. (2023, December 8). *On BECOMING: Goal setting and overcoming imposter syndrome.* Linkedin. https://www.linkedin.com/pulse/becoming-goal-setting-overcoming-imposter-syndrome-oniyitan-rmhgf

Orbe-Austin, L. (2022, September 28). *Vulnerability and compassion are key practices integral to combating your imposter syndrome.* Dynamic Transitions LLP. https://www.dynamictransitionsllp.com/vulnerability-and-compassion-are-key-practices-integral-to-combating-your-imposter-syndrome/

Orbe-Austin, L. (2024, February 2). *Avoid these pitfalls when goal setting when you struggle with imposter syndrome.* Dynamic Transitions LLP. https://www.dynamictransitionsllp.com/imposter-syndrome-goal-setting/

Overcome the battle with the superwoman imposter syndrome. (2023, October 21). Twanna Carter. https://twannacarter.com/overcome-battle-with-superwoman-imposter-syndrome/

Overcoming imposter syndrome: Best practices to confidently grow in your career. (2023, September 18). Just Entrepreneurs. https://justentrepreneurs.co.uk/blog/overcoming-imposter-syndrome-best-practices-to-confidently-grow-in-your-career

Overcoming impostor syndrome. (n.d.). Tony Robbins. Retrieved April 22, 2024, from https://www.tonyrobbins.com/mental-health/overcoming-impostor-syndrome/

Patel, L. (2024, February 1). *Overcoming imposter syndrome: Strategies for building confidence in your career.* Lomit Patel. https://www.lomitpatel.com/articles/overcoming-imposter-syndrome-strategies-for-building-confidence-in-your-career/

Patzak, A., Kollmayer, M., & Schober, B. (2017). Buffering Impostor Feelings with Kindness: The Mediating Role of Self-compassion between Gender-Role Orientation and the Impostor Phenomenon. *Frontiers in Psychology, 8.* https://doi.org/10.3389/fpsyg.2017.01289

Paulise, L. (2023, March 8). *75% of women executives experience imposter syndrome in the workplace.* Forbes. https://www.forbes.com/sites/lucianapaulise/2023/03/08/75-of-women-executives-experience-imposter-syndrome-in-the-workplace/?sh=2e18be136899

Pethkar, J. (2023, April 19). *10 ways to overcome imposter syndrome as a woman founder.* Soror - the Sisters Edit; Sororedit. https://www.sororedit.com/blog/10-ways-to-overcome-imposter-syndrome-as-a-woman-founder/1635

Pigeon, S. (2023, May 2). *How to overcome imposter syndrome and start embracing your successes.* Openspace Clinic. https://openspaceclinic.com/how-to-overcome-imposter-syndrome-and-start-embracing-your-successes/

Pivotal Solutions. (2022, May 27). *HR management: Imposter syndrome, its impact on your team, and what you can do about it.* Pivotal Integrated HR Solutions. https://www.pivotalsolutions.com/imposter-syndrome-and-its-impact-on-hr-management/

Pretorius, E. (2023, September 7). *Embracing imposter syndrome: A catalyst for growth and authentic leadership.* CT: Evolve. https://ct.me/embracing-imposter-syndrome-a-catalyst-for-growth-and-authentic-leadership/

ProDevs. (2023, March 13). *Overcoming imposter syndrome: Tips and strategies for female tech talents.* Linkedin. https://www.linkedin.com/pulse/overcoming-imposter-syndrome-tips-strategies-female-tech

Pryor, H. (2023, September 18). *Imposter syndrome and self-doubt can actually help you build confidence — and even be healthy.* Business Insider. https://www.businessinsider.com/how-imposter-syndrome-can-build-confidence-is-healthy-2023-9

Psychology Today Staff. (2019). *Imposter syndrome.* Psychology Today. https://www.psychologytoday.com/us/basics/imposter-syndrome

Quigley, K. (2024, February 9). *Empowering women: Overcoming imposter syndrome!* Www.linkedin.com. https://www.linkedin.com/pulse/empowering-women-overcoming-imposter-syndrome-khristina-quigley--uhhqe

Ramaswamy, V. (2023, June 5). *The silent struggle: How imposter syndrome affects corporate women.* Linkedin. https://www.linkedin.com/pulse/silent-struggle-how-imposter-syndrome-affects-women-veena-ramaswamy/

Real Life Resilience. (2022, December 2). *Research stats on why imposter syndrome affects female leaders more than men.* Linkedin. https://www.linkedin.com/pulse/research-stats-why-imposter-syndrome-affects-female-/

Reid, S. (n.d.). *Imposter syndrome: Causes, types, and coping tips.* HelpGuide. https://www.helpguide.org/articles/well-being-happiness/imposter-syndrome-causes-types-and-coping-tips.htm

Rouhani, S. (2022, July 1). *Impostor syndrome and self-compassion.* CPTSD Foundation. https://cptsdfoundation.org/2022/07/01/impostor-syndrome-and-self-compassion/

Santos, R. (2024, February 29). *How to overcome impostor syndrome at work.* AirSwift. https://www.airswift.com/blog/how-to-overcome-impostor-syndrome-at-work

Saymeh, A. (2023, February 22). *What is imposter syndrome? Definition, symptoms, and overcoming it.* BetterUp. https://www.betterup.com/blog/what-is-imposter-syndrome-and-how-to-avoid-it

Seltzer, S. M. (2016, February 3). *We Are Being Set Up To Fail — & It Should Make You Mad As Hell.* Refinery29. https://www.refinery29.com/en-us/imposter-syndrome-and-women

Sheryl Sandberg. (2024, April 22). Forbes. https://www.forbes.com/profile/sheryl-sandberg/?sh=3f39fa3d58b6

Simpson, C. (2023, May 5). Author post: How to erase imposter syndrome. *Forbes.* https://www.forbes.com/sites/forbesbooksauthors/2023/05/04/how-to-erase-imposter-syndrome/?sh=47a6f0c86a15

60% of women put off starting a business due to imposter syndrome. (2019, May 15). NatWest Group. https://www.natwestgroup.com/news-and-insights/feature-content/our-updates/2011-2020/60--

of-women-put-off-starting-a-business-due-to-imposter-syndrom.html

Sonya. (n.d.). *Strategies for navigating imposter syndrome as a female leader*. Your Styled Collective. https://www.yourstyledcollective.com.au/blog/navigating-imposter-syndrome

Stanley, K. (2023, July 20). *How CFT can overcome imposter syndrome*. Balanced Minds. https://balancedminds.com/cft-and-imposter-syndrome/

Super Mamas. (2019, December 17). *Episode 220: Setting realistic goals for the new year & getting rid of impostor syndrome with michelle gomez, career & life coach*. Super Mamas. https://supermamas.com/episodeblog/2019/12/16/ep220-setting-realistic-goals-for-the-new-year-and-getting-rid-of-imposter-syndrome-with-michelle-gomez-career-and-life-coach

Sutton, W. (2017, December 11). *Processing my struggle with depression and imposter syndrome in silicon valley*. Linkedin. https://www.linkedin.com/pulse/processing-my-struggle-depression-imposter-syndrome-silicon-sutton

T, R. (2023, January 24). *Stop telling women they have imposter syndrome turns two!* Linkedin. https://www.linkedin.com/pulse/stop-telling-women-have-imposter-syndrome-turns-two-ruchika-tulshyan/

Tan, W. (2023, March 15). *12 easy tips to overcome imposter syndrome*. Flow with Wenlin. https://wenlintan.com/overcome-imposter-syndrome/

Team Guidely. (2023, November 6). *Understanding & overcoming imposter syndrome in 5 easy steps*. Guidely.

https://guidely.com/understanding-overcoming-imposter-syndrome/

The Career Coach. (2023, January 13). *How to overcome "impostor syndrome."* Linkedin. https://www.linkedin.com/pulse/how-overcome-impostor-syndrome-thecareer-coach#:~:text=Practising%20self-compassion%20is%20another

3 reasons we get trapped into self-doubt and imposter syndrome. (2024, January 16). *The Times of India.* https://timesofindia.indiatimes.com/life-style/health-fitness/de-stress/imposter-syndrome-3-reasons-we-get-trapped-into-selfdoubt-and/articleshow/106880879.cms

The Team at Be Your Best Self and Thrive. (2023, October 29). *Mindfulness & overcoming imposter syndrome: Embrace your true worth.* Thrive Counseling. https://www.bybsandthrive.com/post/mindfulness-overcoming-imposter-syndrome

Thornton, T. (2021, April 13). *Imposter syndrome: Why we need to change the conversation.* Linkedin. https://www.linkedin.com/pulse/imposter-syndrome-why-we-need-change-conversation-taz-thornton-

Tulshyan, R., & Burey, J.-A. (2021, February 11). *Stop telling women they have imposter syndrome.* Harvard Business Review. https://hbr.org/2021/02/stop-telling-women-they-have-imposter-syndrome

Understanding and overcoming impostor syndrome. (2023, June 2). McLean Hospital. https://www.mcleanhospital.org/essential/impostor-syndrome

What i'm struggling with: Battling imposter syndrome. (2023, August 8). WomenInDev. https://womenindev.com/what-im-struggling-with-battling-imposter-syndrome/

Wikipedia Contributors. (2019, March 27). *Impostor syndrome.* Wikipedia; Wikimedia Foundation. https://en.wikipedia.org/wiki/Impostor_syndrome

Wilson, I. (2020, August 26). *Why imposter syndrome has a greater impact on women and women of color.* Linkedin. https://www.linkedin.com/pulse/why-imposter-syndrome-has-greater-impact-women-colour-ingrid/

Wodarczak, S. (2023, March 13). *Women, careers, academia, and the imposter syndrome.* New Wave Magazine. https://www.newwavezine.com/post/women-careers-academia-and-the-imposter-syndrome

Women@SCS. (2020, October 9). *Overcoming imposter syndrome.* Medium. https://medium.com/@womenatscs/overcoming-imposter-syndrome-e24a92f088c2

Yoni. (2023, July 12). *Conquering imposter syndrome: Embracing your true potential.* Yoni Healing. https://www.yonihealing.co.za/blogs/news/conquering-imposter-syndrome-embracing-your-true-potential

www.ingramcontent.com/pod-product-compliance
Lightning Source LLC
Chambersburg PA
CBHW050058230526
45470CB00004B/1587